ST. SIMONS ISLAND

R. Edwin Green

FIRST EDITION

Seventh Printing 1994

PRINTED IN THE UNITED STATES OF AMERICA

second printing 1983
third printing 1985
fourth printing 1987
fifth printing 1989
sixth printing 1992

**LIBRARY OF CONGRESS
CATALOG CARD NO.: 82-70251**

**Green, R. Edwin
St. Simons Island**

**Rome, NY: Arner Publications
90 p.**
8201   **820119**

ISBN 0914124102

ST. SIMONS ISLAND

a summary of its history

by

R. Edwin Green

Illustrated by Mary A. Green

PURPOSE

This book is written for the person who would like to read a simple, accurate account of the various historic periods of St. Simons Island, Georgia. There have been many fine books of history already written, each of which has its importance. Some describe the entire coastal area of Georgia and the past of each of the islands. For the new reader of island history, however, the reading of so many accounts tends to be confusing. Other histories give major attention to one period of time, or one event, or one place. This is valuable for a study in depth, but for the visitor or casual reader, it is probably more than he wants to know.

Furthermore, it is also easy for the new reader to become confused. Since names are similar in different generations and families of the island intermarry and also sell land to each other, one important event may be in an entirely different time period than another.

This writing is my effort, after reading the various histories, to "sort it out", so that the visitor, the new resident, or the person with an awakened interest in our historic past can quickly read an outline story of St. Simons Island, Georgia.

It is my hope that the reader will become so interested in one or more of these historic periods, that he or she will go to various books which cover the period or event in greater depth.

Life on this island will be much more interesting if you know who lived here before, what they did, why it was important. There is no place the size of this little island which has had any more varied and interesting past than this island to which you visit or on which you live. May this writing lead to your fuller appreciation of it.

I express sincere thanks to Mrs. Mildred Frazier, president of the Coastal Georgia Historical Society, to Mrs. Betty Bryde, curator of the Methodist Museum at Epworth-by-the Sea, and to others, who have evaluated this manuscript and made helpful suggestions.

R. Edwin Green
St. Simons Island, Georgia
1982

TABLE OF CONTENTS

The historic eras of St. Simons Island, Georgia

(The author suggests that it will be helpful if you have read the preceding pages listing the historic periods and purpose of this book.)

I. THE ISLAND AND THE INDIANS

In the long ages past, when the planet Earth was in the process of creation, even then, the area of the earth we know as coastal Georgia was an ancient island. The first ancestor of our present island was a land mass which geologists have called "Appalachia". This had nothing to do with the present Appalachian mountains, for this was before their formation. At that time they were at the bottom of a huge continental trough filled with sea water and being ever loaded with land material eroding from both the land masses on the west and the island of Appalachia on the east.

This great primeval island, over 500 million years ago, extended from the present Gulf of Mexico to Maryland, from the present mountains to the east edge of the continental shelf. For 200 million years it remained so, until gradually it elongated to the north end and became attached to the continent. Now as a peninsula the sun rose and set for another 100 million years, until gradually the island became a part of the continent as the mountain ranges were born.

Even as it became part of the continent, the ocean shore line remained in its original position for 50 million years. Then at some early time a melting of the polar glaciers caused the waters of the Atlantic Ocean to invade the land and to cover it to the place which geologists call the Fall Line. This extends across Georgia from Columbus through Macon, Milledgeville, and Augusta. With successive warming and cooling trends of the earth across the ages, this land was successively covered and uncovered by the sea. Deposits of ocean sediment covered the ancient island, so today one would have to drill four or five thousand feet to reach the rock of the original island of Appalachia.

The present coast line was established in the steps of creation during the last ice age, known as the Wisconsin freeze, 25,000 years ago. This Wisconsin freeze and its subsequent thawing was the immediate cause of our present sea islands. As the ice melted and the waters rose, there were at first similar islands to the east with salt marsh on the seaward side of our present islands. As the waters further rose our present land is the top of sedimentary rock stacked in layers on the remains of this the most ancient island; then as the continental glaciers melted, our islands were separated from the mainland.

Of course, this is recent geological history of perhaps only 1000 years ago. Some students of ocean geology believe that another glacial melt began in 1920 and calculate that the rise in Atlantic waters will be 1½ feet a century. If so, and if the trend continues, in another thousand years one could witness the emergence of areas of the coastal mainland as the new islands of the sea. Of course, the trend could change in the other direction at any time as well.

Before turning to the emergence of man upon these islands, there are three other physical features of which we should be aware.

The first is our source of fresh water. On an island, surrounded by the salt water of the sea and the brackish water of the creeks and rivers, even on a hot, almost rainless summer, how can enough fresh water be drawn for thousands of homes, large industries, watering of lawns and golf courses? Where does so much fresh water come from? The answer is artesian wells. Hundreds of miles away in the mountains, water enters into a stratum of porous rock which outcrops to the surface. This porous rock when underground runs between layers of impervious rock, both below and above, through which little water can escape. It then gradually moves downhill from the mountain and coastal plain through the porous rock until at some lower level it again outcrops as a large spring or until it can be tapped by a drilled well, which is a man made spring. The greatest portion of the water has a rate of movement through the rock of less then ten feet a day, so it would take water two or three hundred years from entering as rain in the mountains until it is tapped for use in the coastal islands. For example, in 1885 a great flowing artesian well was dug at St. Simons Mills by the Dodge, Meigs & Co. lumber mills. It was 437 feet deep with a flow of 200 gallons per minute through a six inch pipe. The water rose in a stand pipe 38 feet above the ground and flowed into a reservoir as high as the top of the mill. This gave sufficient force for fire fighting as well as water for mill work and fresh drinking water. Concern is now arising in the present time a century later, that heavy industrial use and increased population is drawing out the water more rapidly than its flow can replenish; brackish water then creeps in. Therefore, sources of fresh water such as the rivers are being considered in order to conserve from the artesian wells.

The second physical feature of interest is the relative freedom of St. Simons Island and its area from the most destructive force of hurricanes. Although even a small hurricane is too much, the winds over Georgia's coastal islands are much less vicious than at most other places. In the past 200 years there have been only four or five of consequence, and they were small compared to many occurring at places both north and south of here. Only one took many lives: that of 1804 when about 100 Negro slaves crossing the Hampton river in open boats were drowned. In 1898 a large portion of St. Simons Island was flooded by a hurricane wind that heaped up a high rise of water to about five feet above the marshes. It was no surge or wall of water, but a rise from wind sustained tides. The water receded in a very few hours, having chiefly damaged livestock caught on the marshes.

The explanation of St. Simons' relative freedom from hurricanes is related to the Gulf Stream. Brunswick is the mid-point of an arc with Miami on the south and Cape Hatteras on the north. The Gulf Stream somewhat follows the concavity of the shore line. It is closest to land at Palm Beach and Cape Hatteras. It is farthest from the shore opposite St. Simons Island, where it is a distance of 80 miles. Hurricanes breed in the Caribbean and then move into the low atmospheric pressure areas of the heated surfaces of the southern states. Florida is the nearest large land area to their breeding grounds, therefore they bend their course toward the peninsula. They may hurdle across into the Gulf of Mexico, where they may turn north into the Gulf states or head back to Florida and out into the Atlantic. Here they are caught in a mighty trap — the heated area over the 50 mile wide Gulf Stream forms a long corridor of light air between two walls of heavier air. It is along this corridor that the hurricane travels northward. Thus it passes only within 80 miles of St. Simons Island. Since it passes St. Simons Island on its left as it moves northward, St. Simons lies in the less dangerous semi-circle of the hurricane and the winds over Georgia's islands are less vicious than they would be on lands that might lie on the right side in the more dangerous winds.

Also concerning the weather, it should be noted that during the summer the area is under the influence of the Bermuda High, laying off to the east. This prevents the usual progression of Hi and Low pressures from moving through in normal progression. Thus, in summer the weather is subject to local thunderstorms, rather than to the large system of atmospheric movement. Of course this is no longer effective in the hurricane season, and as fall comes near, the pattern of weather movement returns to normal.

Local winds are caused by the differential heating of the air over land and water — the land and sea breezes. Land heats more rapidly than does water by the sun's rays; and similarly the land cools more rapidly with the coming of night or winter. Therefore, in summer the land near the seashore is heated more rapidly than the water. The heated air on land flows upward being lighter, and the cooler heavier air of the sea moves in to fill the place. This is the sea breeze. Also from this we have clouds or thunder clouds almost every summer afternoon as the rising hot air becomes chilled and its moisture is condensed. Usually the breezes blow from the sea to the land from about noon to perhaps one o'clock a.m., when the process is reversed by the sea being by then warmer than the land.

Fogs also spring from a difference in temperature. Just as dew or frost is formed on a still night by radiation of heat from the ground, so is ground fog formed in their stead if the air should be stirred by a very slight breeze. Smoking streams on a cold morning is an example of ground fog. When warm air moves over a colder ground surface, such as wind blowing from a warmer sea to land on a cold night, there would develop an advection fog. A frontal fog is just a cloud on the ground. Although fogs plague many coastal areas, it is not a severe problem in the St. Simons Island area for there are no extreme differences in temperature between land and sea.

The third noteworthy physical feature is the marsh. Twice a day bathed in sea water with the rising and falling of the tide, it has developed a unique life of its own. Fertile in its production of protein from marsh grasses and marine life, it enriches the ocean water and plays an important part in the food chain of the sea and land as well.

The Indians

Into this fertile island of wilderness beauty and mild climate, at some time in the long ago, man made his appearance. Doubtless, Indians lived on the mainland before the time the coastal islands emerged from the sea. Then as the dry land appeared with beaches, dunes, and forests, the mainland Indians may have been the first vacationists. Indian canoes probably bore individuals, and later whole tribes for hunting and fishing on these islands. Then some remained and villages were begun. Little has been known about the aboriginal inhabitants between Savannah and the St. John river, until fortunately some progress was made since 1936 when the construction of the airport on St. Simons uncovered bones and skulls from grave sites and a village site. Archeologists recommended by the Smithsonian took over the excavation work to reveal important information. Over 21,000 artifacts including 35 bone or stone awls were found at the site near the airport. Approximately 3,000 post molds and some evidence of clay floors were located, indicating the large number of dwellings included in this village. Soon work and bits of pottery indicated burials before 1500, for after that date beads and bits of bright-hued glass brought by the white traders are nearly always found at Indian sites. On practically every bluff on St. Simons were shell banks which were the refuse heaps or "kitchen middens" of the Indians. They contained oyster and clam shells, broken pottery, bones of animals eaten by these Indians, bowls, drinking vessels, hoes and tools fashioned from conch and whelk shells, awls and other tools made of animal and bird bones.

These Indians were Creeks of Muskhogean stock. In figure they were tall, well shaped; their manners were dignified; their countenance open and placid, with heroism and bravery stamped on their brows. Their complexion was reddish brown, and their long coarse hair was deep black. In their actions they exhibited an air of independence and superiority. The men were very ambitious of conquest, warfare seeming to be the men's favorite pastime, but were ever magnanimous to a vanquished foe.

These Creek Indians occupying the coastal plains were far from being savages. They were politically well organized, occupied permanent villages, and were largely engaged in the cultivation of corn, beans, melons, and fruit. Tobacco was cultivated and universally used, the Indians believing that smoking was peculiarly pleasing to the Great Spirit, whom they fancied was himself addicted to this habit. The pipe was their constant companion — their solace in fatigue and trouble, their delight in hours of ease.   It was a symbol of peace and friendship, and was also used in religious and political rites. Large, highly ornamented pipes, called "calumets" were employed only on occasions of ceremony. Just as among the white man it was an emblem of peace and good-will to drink from the same cup, so it was a similar idea of the Indians to take a whiff from the same pipe. The Indians regarded corn as a direct gift from the Great Spirit, and observed festivals with interesting ceremonies both when it was planted and gathered.

Their villages were crude cabins made of upright poles daubed with earth, leaves, or moss. The dwelling of the chief or mico was usually in the center of the village and was larger and more carefully finished than the houses of the common people. Next to warfare, hunting was the favorite pastime of the men, although the men assisted in making crops and in other outdoor work, so that all the drudgery was not left to the women, as was the case in some other areas. Dogs were domesticated, abounded in all their villages, and were constant companions and friends of their masters.

Of course the Creek Indians were divided into many

tribes or provinces. The territory between St. Catherines and St. Andrews Sounds was the province of Guale (pronounced "Wallie"), taking its name from an old Indian chief Guale, who resided on Saint Catherine Island. As the Indians moved about they attached their names to any piece of land they occupied, until all this territory was called Guale. Even the waters between St. Simons Island and Jekyll Island the Indians called Gualauini, meaning the waters of Guale.

Each village was governed by a chief or "mico". There was also a "mico mayer" or head chief, exercising a sort of lordship over the other chieftains. Reports indicate that this coastal area was relatively well populated, with from twenty-two to forty villages. Since the Gualeans sometimes relocated their villages, it is difficult to know the exact number or to locate their exact sites. In all probability the Indians carried their village name along with them as they moved from one site to another. The southern villages around St. Simons Island seemed to number about eleven. Tolomato seems to have been the head village and the residence of the "mico mayer". Its site was near Darien. Some think it was five miles from Darien on the road beyond the Ridge on Pease Creek at a place known as "The Thicket", where there are some tabby ruins once thought to be remains of a Spanish mission. Later opinion places Tolomato on the bluff in front of the present Fort King George visitors center where excavation found both Indian and Spanish material. Since the Indians were mobile, the village Tolomato may have had various locations, while still remaining the head village and the residence of the mico mayer.

Thus these natives, breathing the soft air of a genial climate and surrounded by forests and streams that supplied them food with little effort, were relieved in great measure from any severe struggle for clothes and shelter. On a whole, these Creek Indians were a gentle, agricultural people, with pleasure-loving dispositions. With no thought of change, they lived simple lives, unconscious of civilization on the far side of the great waters and unknowing of the pale-faced warriors who would bring great changes to their way of life.

POSSIBLE SITES OF SPANISH MISSIONS

II. THE SPANISH MISSIONS

The first European explorer to visit Georgia was Hernando De Soto. He sailed from Cuba in 1539 to Florida, then in 1540 made his way into Georgia with 620 soldiers, eight priests, and several dozen huge dogs trained for battle. Claiming what is now coastal Georgia for Spain, he then made his way through present South Carolina, Alabama, and Mississippi; then dying enroute in 1542.

The French were the first to start colonization. In 1562 French Hugenots, led by Ribault, made a settlement at Ft. Royal, S.C., which was soon abandoned. Two years later another settlement, led by Loudonierre, was made on the south bank of the St. Johns river in Florida and called Ft. Caroline.

These French settlements on land which Spain considered to be hers aroused Spanish anger. So Spain sent her most able seaman, Pedro Menendez de Avilles, to rout the French and to hold the lands for Spain. He established St. Augustine as a base, and in the following year, 1566, made a trip up the Georgia coast and landed on the island of St. Catherines. Here he found an old Indian chief named Guale (pronounced ''Wallie'') with whom he made friends. He wrote that they ''sat on the beach and ate biscuits and honey''. Leaving his nephew and a few other Spaniards there, he departed to return a few weeks later with a group of fifty people for a settlement at that place. This was the first of a string of Spanish settlements which he made. His agents in the new territory were the priest and the soldier. His strategy was to found a series of missions, with the pious intention of converting the Indians to the Christian faith, but with the soldiers present to protect the mission. Thus, the land would be effectively held for Spain.

This opportunity of beginning missions to convert the heathen Indians was greeted with enthusiasm by the pious King Philip II of Spain. He selected the Jesuits for the honor, and on July 28, 1566, three priests of strong character set sail. However, tragedy marked this endeavor from the beginning. Near the coast of Florida, a violent storm separated their ship from the others and they drifted northward, lost and without food. In desperation they went ashore on what is now Cumberland Island. At first the Indians gave them food, but then turned hostile. Father Pedro Martinez refused to flee immediately as some of the Flemish sailors would have been abandoned there to certain death. Delaying too long, they were attacked by forty Indians with bows and arrows. Father Martinez was surrounded, and since his deep religious conviction prevented him from fighting, he raised his hands and face to the skies in prayer. In that instant an Indian with a club crushed his head beneath the upraised supplicating hands. So this priest became the first Christian martyr on Georgia soil. Three Flemish sailors shared the same fate, the remainder of the party getting back to the ship and making escape.

Yet, by force of arms and missionary persistence, missions were established along the coast. One of the priests, Brother Domingo Agustin Baez, applied himself to learning the language of the Indians and is said to have written a grammar of the language and translated a catechism for their instruction. This was the first book ever written on U.S. soil. Before the end of the year, however, he succumbed during an epidemic — the second priest to die as a martyr of the faith on the Georgia soil.

The priests worked hard at their task, but in spite of this, their early efforts bore disappointing results. The mission buildings would be erected near Indian villages, but the Indians did not want to stay near the mission where they could be instructed. It was their habit to move about, planting on better land. But once moved, the friars couldn't find them for instruction, so they tried to keep them in one place by creating a town and giving them corn to plant. This did not produce the hoped for success. The Indians seemed to desire escape from the domination of the priest and the plans the church had for them, so they would soon be gone. There was also a theological misunderstanding. In the course of the sermons to instruct the natives on the doctrine of the Holy Trinity, the motive for the Adoration of the Cross (to which the natives seemed to respond with devotion), the priest declared that to be sons of God it was necessary to be enemies of the devil, who was the essence of evil. The Indians misunderstood this. They thought the reference was to one of their own gods and were highly incensed. The devil, they said, was the best thing in the world because it made men fearless and brave.

Increasing misunderstanding and conflict between the friars and the natives and martyrdom and punishment brought the Jesuit effort to a close. By 1570 most missions were deserted, and in 1572 the remaining friars were ordered to service in Mexico.

The Spanish king did not give up easily, so soon the ill fated work of the Jesuits was taken over by the Franciscans. In 1573 a few Franciscans arrived, but apathy at home delayed the real effort until 1593. By this time it was recognized that soldiers must accompany the friars to their posts and substantial buildings must be erected as mission stations. Rapidly a whole chain of mission stations was founded along the coast, individual stations being in the principal Indian villages of Guale.

A mission was established at the important Indian village of Tolomato by Pedro Ruiz in 1595. This was near the present Darien. Recent historians mark the site as the bluff directly opposite the visitors center at Fort King George, as both Indian and Spanish material was found there during excavations. Earlier writers had placed the site as "The Thicket", five miles northeast where some old tabby ruins had been found. Those advocating the Fort King George site claim that the mission buildings in this area were of wooden construction, not tabby.

Sub-mission stations were located on St. Simons Island: 1) Asao or San Simon, near the present ruins of Ft. Frederica; 2) Ocotonico, between the lighthouse and the Frederica river; and 3) Santo Domingo de Talaxe, inland from the junction of the Frederica and Hampton rivers, near Butler Point. (Old maps and historians do not always agree as to the exact location of the missions. Some place this one as San Buenaventura and put Santo Domingo on the mainland.)

The Mission Asao was in the charge of Father Velascola, a giant of a man from the mountains of Cantabria. His simple humility, combined with his powerful physique, made a deep impression on the natives of Asao (St. Simons Island) and vicinity. The Franciscans brought their inexorable discipline. Without trying to teach the Indians the use of Latin or Castilian, the friar immediately began instruction in the native language through an interpreter, until he himself gained a mastery of it. The Latin of the ritual was not dispensed with however; each day began with saying prayers, devotional and Mass at least once a week, until the new converts were quite proficient in the ritual of the faith.

This was a period of success, and as the missions prospered the governor was anxious to expand the effort to occupy other rich lands and save the souls of the natives. In 1606 the Bishop of Cuba made the first pastoral visit ever made on U.S. soil. He visited the missions at San Pedro, Tazale, Espogache, and Santa Cataline and baptized 1070 neophytes.

Although the Spanish missions flourished in the early 17th century, this had not always been accomplished with ease. This is very evident in the story of the Juanillo Revolt in this very area of Guale of which this history is concerned.

The friars brought Spanish and Christian customs and often pressed for conformity from the Indians who little understood them. The natives were at best considered wards with a "priest knows best" attitude, and at worst were often treated more like slaves. A particular bitterness was encountered at Tolomato where Father Corpa had reproached the Indians harshly for disobeying his injunction that they should have only one wife.

The many items of dissatisfaction broke out into real trouble in 1597 when it came time for Juanillo, the son of the chief of Guale, to become "mico mayer". This position was the head chief over the various villages and their local mico chiefs. The position of mico mayer did not seem to be automatically hereditary, for sometimes nephews or others were selected instead of sons of the former chief. Yet here at Tolomato, Juanillo was in line for the head mico position, but Father Corpa intervened effectively to deprive him of it. Seeing Juanillo as an

FATHER VELASCOLA was the Spanish missionary at Mission Asao on St. Simons Island. In 1597, during an Indian revolt, he was ambushed and killed. In the painting Father Velascola, a large and strong man from the mountains of Spain, is depicted surrounded by his dream of Christian missions.

exceedingly arrogant, quarrelsome, and warlike young Indian, who refused to obey his commands on many occasions, Father Corpa appointed as head mico an older man "with good humble habits," which the Spanish overlords preferred.

Juanillo was greatly incensed at this and gathered a large group of other malcontents into revolt. They first murdered Father Corpa as he came to the church for his morning devotions, and then the next day addressed a large gathering of chiefs of surrounding tribes. Playing upon the prejudices and their feeling of oppression, he boasted of the killing of the padre and pictured the friars as the great destroyers of Indian customs and happiness. The tribes of Guale were so stirred up by this that they embarked on raids and murder at most of the missions in Guale. Even at Asao (St. Simons), where Father Velascola was such a large and powerful man physically, they individually being afraid of him, awaited his return from St. Augustine to ambush him and cut his body beyond recognition.

Such a widespread revolt could not be ignored by the Spanish. This undercut their hopes of both holding the coast and exploiting the interior. So Indian atrocity was met by Spanish atrocity. The soldiers hunted out Indians to punish and were often frustrated and angered by the easy way the Indians vanished into the wilderness out of sight. So they burned their crops, and in the destruction were aided by a drought that summer, creating a real food shortage. Indian village after Indian village was burned, and the suffering increased.

Gradually the less violent of the tribes subsided in their hatred of the missionaries, particularly in return for badly needed food. So now with many Indians as ally, the Spanish pressed for order and rule again. The chief of Asao led Indians of many villages to an attack on a fortified town in the interior, Yfusinique, where Juanillo and his followers had retreated. The rebels fought with strength and desperation, but were finally overrun by a great general assault. Finding the bodies of Juanillo and his ally Don Francisco, they took their scalps, and later exhibited these scalps in St. Augustine as a sign of Spanish victory.

So the missions were rebuilt and continued to flourish

and expand, holding the land peacefully again for Spain for the next seventy or eighty years. By 1667 mission bells were heard all over Guale, for the record of 1667 shows that there were seventy missions and forty missionaries in Guale.

Yet time and world politics bring changes. In 1670 the English founded Charleston, and in the coming years the English became a new menace to the missions and the Spanish settlements of the New World.

Soon after the founding of Charleston, England and Spain had made a treaty by which the principle of actual occupation was adopted as the policy for colonization. English ownership was legalized as far south as Charleston and Spanish claims as far north as Santa Elene Sound. But almost immediately there developed a sharp conflict between Spain and England for the "debatable land", a conflict which was to last for three-quarters of a century, culminating in the military decision at the Battle of Bloody Marsh.

In 1675 the missions were flourishing, but as the years passed they were to be put under increased pressure. As always there was some dissatisfaction and misunderstanding between the friars and the Indians, especially where the priest was very arbitrary and demanding. This hostility was greatly enhanced by the English, anxious to replace the Spanish in the area. So the English increasingly played on Indian dissatisfaction to stir up trouble and bring conflict between dissatisfied tribes and the loyal mission Indians.

Also, pirates became a problem for the missions. Pirates raided and sacked them time and again. In this they were doubtlessly encouraged and even supplied by the English in South Carolina as a part of the pressure on the Spanish. These pirate raids would destroy the mission, carry off the valuables including the mission bells, soon silencing their call to worship forever. Under these pressures the Spanish gradually withdrew until by 1686 most missions of Guale had been abandoned.

In this period the population of Indians had also declined. The interruption of their normal life and hunting grounds, warfare, various new diseases, and great numbers leaving for other lands probably all contributed to this decline. The number of villages declined from sixty-six to a low of six or seven. A list made at St. Augustine of Indians who could bear arms produced only 122 names from a total population of 417 in nine villages. Meager were the remains of the "thirty thousand" Indians originally on the Georgia-Florida coast.

Thus, this region of Guale of which we are most concerned — St. Simons, Sea Island, Jekyll, Darien — now abandoned by the Spanish and only sparsely populated by Indians, had a period of around fifty years in which nature took its course unhindered again by man.

III. THE ENGLISH PERIOD

In 1732 King George II of England signed a charter authorizing the establishing of a colony in America between South Carolina and the Spanish territory of Florida "for the settling of the poor persons of London". Although this altruistic motive was real, and helped in raising funds for the venture, there was also adequate military reason for the new settlement. Spanish ships were harassing trade with the colonies. The firm entrenchment of the Spanish in Florida, with hostile Indians under their control, was evidence that the Spanish would push on north as rapidly as possible, thereby threatening English colonies one by one. Ignoring an old treaty giving them colonization rights only as far south as Charleston, they emphasized that just because the Spanish had a few missions along the Georgia coast a century before was no firm claim on this land now.

So a colony was authorized in 1732, and just the right man volunteered to lead the party which would pioneer the settling of Georgia — James Edward Oglethorpe.

The young Oglethorpe, now only age 35, had already distinguished himself, first as a soldier and then as a member of Parliament. He was known for his honesty, truthfulness, and as a moderate and wise legislator. This fine reputation had been enhanced by his service on a committee to investigate England's debtors' prisons. He had found that most of the prisoners were not criminals. A great depression, following years of war and government waste, had caused many to overextend their credit. Thus, many otherwise respected citizens were confined in prison for debt. They were confined there for an indefinite period of time, unless somehow they could bribe their way to freedom. Wardens often arranged good meals and clean quarters for a price, but if a debtor could not pay, he might receive very inhuman treatment. Most debtors

PERIOD OF FORT FREDERICA

were in filth, in damp cells, ánd often starving and ill. There were stories of prisoners being tortured to death so the warden could confiscate their personal belongings. Oglethorpe's distress at conditions became more personal when he found a friend of his living in such conditions. This young architect, now completely out of money to buy favors, suffered under fear of being sent to a prison building into an epidemic of smallpox. Oglethorpe could hardly believe such a thing could happen, but alas, even his pleas to the warden were without avail.

These investigations by Oglethorpe and his committee brought out even worse horrors, which were made in a detailed report to Parliament. This resulted in a reform of prison conditions and management, and led to the enactment of the Debtors Act, where for the first time in English history the rights of a debtor were protected. This law was a great achievement, and helped establish the reputation of James Oglethorpe all over England.

Thus, when a leader was needed for a new colony across the Atlantic, James Oglethorpe was just the person. Here was the opportunity for a new experiment. Could the issues for which he had fought in Parliament be proven practical and worthy in a new setting, in a new society unspoiled by inherited prejudice and debasing competition?

The Trustees of the colony saw this as an opportunity to give people — poor and unemployed because there was no work — a fresh start. Once they became established and self-sufficient, their industry and success would bring much needed trade and wealth to the Crown.

So with the reputation of Oglethorpe and the altruistic purposes of the project, the colony of Georgia became a household word. Financial backers were easily secured. The trustees carefully selected the first settlers to go. Only the most responsible and ambitious of the applicants were given preference. All of them had permission of their creditors to go; none were deserting wives and families. Even on the day of sailing, each family was called before the trustees, asked if they were satisfied with the arrangements, and given a chance to back out and remain in London.

It was November, 1732. On the 200 ton frigate **Anne**

there were 114 emigrants, along with General Oglethorpe, a doctor, an engineer, and a druggist. The **Volant** was loaded with freight and also carried an additional four immigrants.

Although lashed by the Atlantic winter gales, the ships made anchor in Charles Town harbor safely. Two infants had died during the voyage, but the rest of the immigrants revived quickly once on Carolina soil. They were welcomed warmly by the Charleston governor and people, who gave them ample provisions, and would provide boats and guides for the rest of the journey. Oglethorpe lost no time in inspecting the lands to the south, and selected a bluff on the Savannah river for his new colony. Wisely, he made contact with the Indians and worked out permission with them for a settlement here. It was his good fortune to find a half-Indian woman who had gone to school in the Carolinas and spoke English. This Mary Musgrove was the daughter-in-law of Colonel John Musgrove, who had been sent into this area several years before to negotiate trade with the natives. Mrs. Musgrove's large influence with the Indians made her service invaluable. She and her husband were immediately hired as interpreters and go-betweens with her tribe.

Boats were rented in Charleston, and the settlers moved to the new site of the colony, arriving at Savannah on February 12, 1733. Working with great energy, they cleared the land and built the town, and such good progress had been made by early 1734 that Oglethorpe felt free to explore the rest of the territory to the south, which he also claimed for the English crown.

He spotted a point of high land along the western shore of St. Simons Island, about halfway up the island where the river curved somewhat concealing it. Just the place for a fort! A fort was needed for defense against the Spanish who still thought this territory was theirs. Of course, Oglethorpe had to go back to England to convince the Trustees of the need to build a fort, since he had quite arbitrarily extended the Georgia boundary southward.

Arriving back in England, he was welcomed home with great enthusiasm. The Red Men he took with him, in native costumes, with strange sounding names, caused a sensation. Poems were written in their honor, a medal was struck to commemorate the visit and celebrations were

Drawing of the first shelters at Frederica after the sketches of Von Reck, 1736.

held by nobility and common folk alike.

Oglethorpe did have several fences to mend. There had been criticism of his prohibition of rum, brandy, and other distilled spirits; and to his objection to the introduction of negro slavery into the colony. After all, these were of much profit to business and to the Crown! Yet, with eloquent presentation to Parliament of the problems brought by drink and slavery, and with the further consideration that in a military outpost everyone should bear arms (prohibited to slaves), an agreement was ratified to continue these prohibitions. Some dissatisfaction of the Trustees with the accounting of their funds was allayed when they found that Oglethorpe had expended his own fortune for the colony, proof enough of his honesty. They did deem it wise to send along a secretary to keep better records and to provide them with more complete information than they had been receiving.

King George shared Oglethorpe's vision of Georgia's potential. The Trustees renewed their support now that they had heard first hand of the success of the colony. So now James Oglethorpe could again leave for America. This time the task ahead was a military one if he was to challenge the Spanish. Settlers for this new, exposed, frontier location need be trustworthy and industrious. They need have a variety of useful crafts and talents such as carpenter, blacksmith, farmer, doctor, shoemaker. The trustees seemed to prefer Salzburgers (persecuted Protestants from Germany) and Scottish Highlanders. So it was, that a carefully selected group of forty families — about 230 persons, only a few more than one-third of them men — arrived off Peeper Island (later known as Cockspur Island) in the mouth of the Savannah river in February, 1736.

A problem arose when some of the Salzburgers displayed a reluctance to move on to the new settlement, pleading that warfare was against their religion and fighting in a military settlement might be unavoidable. They really preferred to join the community of their own people

at Ebenezer. Other settlers were reluctant to continue when they discovered the remainder of the voyage must be in very small boats.

Believing it unwise to take anyone to his new military outpost who did not want to go, Oglethorpe again recruited from among them, holding out no false promises, for the hardships would be greater and the location more dangerous.

Finding the affairs in Savannah going well, Oglethorpe lost little time in getting down to St. Simons Island, his site for a new town and fort.

So it was, under great moss-draped live oaks, over-looking the river and acre after acre of marshes, Oglethorpe named the town Frederica in honor of the Prince of Wales, Frederick Louis. With plans for a typically English village and fort, he immediately began construction of the fort. Twenty men were assigned to construction, ten to digging the ditch that must surround the fort. The dirt was to be thrown up as a rampart, and being sandy, must be tufted to prevent erosion. Each person had a job to do and a deadline for its completion.

By March, 1736, forty-four men and seventy-two women and children had begun life in the new town. Each freeholder had a lot for house and garden along the main street. There was also a large public garden inland from

the town, a meadow for cattle, and two wells. Since the Trustees had chosen the colonists for their skill, Frederica was to be a self-sustaining community. There was a doctor, a constable, a carpenter, a baker, a shoemaker, a boatman, a bricklayer, a locksmith. Before long the fort was completed; as soon as possible the thatched houses were replaced by brick and wood homes. Within a very short time Frederica was an industrious, mostly self-contained society.

To give further military strength, an outpost, Fort St. Simons, was built on the south end of the island, and for communications was connected to Frederica by a military road. By this road following the east shore of the island, it was concealed from the Frederica river on the west.

Among the immigrants which Mr. Oglethorpe brought from England were two young ministers who afterwards became very famous. John Wesley, fresh from Oxford University, came as a missionary to the Indians and a pastor to the colonists. His brother, Charles Wesley, was to serve as a private secretary to Oglethorpe. John took up his work in Savannah, making only an occasional trip to Frederica, while Charles came immediately with Oglethorpe to Frederica. His assigned task was to keep records and make reports to the Trustees, a previous failing of Mr. Oglethorpe. He soon discovered that pastoral responsibilities were his as well, so he conducted religious services and organized the settlers into a congregation which still today exists as the continuing congregation of Christ Church.

The Wesley brothers remained only a few months in the colony, however, as they really were not suited for the task. The Indians were no more interested in converting to the Church of England as Christians than they had been interested in accepting Spanish Catholic Christianity a century before. The colonists did not care for the "high church" ritual of their services, and especially did not like arbitrary and unbending moral authority. So, being discouraged by lack of success and disheartened by conflict with too many of the colonists, they were glad to return to the more familiar and settled life in England.

There were two things though which made the Georgia

experience of the Wesleys of great significance: 1) On shipboard and in the colony they had been greatly impressed by the Moravian immigrants. Their trusting faith and deep piety made a deep impression on them, and the future "warm hearted" religious experience and the Methodist movement were greatly influenced by this

Hawkins-Davison Houses
(Sketch from Fort Frederica drawing)

Moravian contact. 2) The first Sunday School in the world was established in Savannah by John Wesley. He brought children together on Sunday for religious instruction. This is not to take away from Robert Raikes, who is given credit for the beginning of the Sunday School movement many years later. Robert Raikes developed an important system of teaching poor children on Sunday. These children had been working in the factories or mines for long hours six days a week, so on Sunday he got them together to teach them reading, writing, and arithmetic, for this was their only opportunity to learn. But the first known instance of getting children together on Sunday for religious instruction was by John Wesley in Savannah, Georgia.

So, although the Wesley brothers were in the colony for only a few months, it was a learning, growing, maturing experience which became part of the foundation upon which the Methodist movement was to be built.

With the colony firmly established and prospering, General Oglethorpe could then turn to asserting the English claim to the territory. England's claim rested upon the discoveries of Sebastian Cabot, who had sailed along this coast long before Spain claimed it as a part of Florida and colonized it with missions over a century before. However, England and Spain were quarreling not only over territory, but over trade, free shipping, and many other grievances. Oglethorpe, seeing war as inevitable, recruited six hundred fifty soldiers in England, carefully selecting them from respectable classes and permitting wives to come along in order to induce them to become permanent settlers. He also made special effort to make friends with the Indians in order to have them as allies.

England did declare war on Spain in 1739, and the next year Oglethorpe was ordered to secure the help of South Carolina and make an invasion of Florida. So he made an expedition against St. Augustine. However, he found it more heavily fortified than he had expected as he laid seige to it. After several weeks without success, some Spanish galleys succeeded in running the gauntlet and carrying fresh supplies to the fort. This, together with his troops being enfeebled by sickness, made him decide it wise to raise the seige and retire.

For the next two years the Spanish acted only on the

defensive; however, Oglethorpe knew they were really gathering forces to retaliate. When the Spanish came to attack, they did have a formidable force of fifty-two vessels and about three thousand men, under the command of Dan Manuel de Montiano, Governor of St. Augustine.

This was a time of great peril for Georgia as this great fleet appeared off St. Simons bar with the intention of taking Frederica. The governor of South Carolina would render no assistance, so General Oglethorpe was put upon his own resources. He had only one small ship, two guard schooners, and some small trading vessels, plus two land batteries at Fort St. Simons on the south end of the island. He had about 650 men.

Seeing it hopeless to hold Fort St. Simons, he withdrew before an attack in order to concentrate all his forces at Frederica. Thus, the Spanish immediately occupied Fort St. Simons. It didn't then take them long to find the military road which led up the island to Frederica, and a detachment made it to within a few miles of the town before the alarm was given. Quickly moving into action, a few rangers and Highlander troops attacked the Spanish with such force that they were temporarily routed. While General Oglethorpe returned to Frederica for additional aid, the Spanish reinforcements poured in and the English company was driven back. The Highlanders, bringing up the rear of the retreat, wheeled aside and concealed themselves in a grove of palmettoes, where they laid an ambush for the pursuing Spaniards.

Reaching this bend in the road and observing the footprints in the sand showing the English in rapid retreat, they concluded that the fighting was over for the day. They stacked their guns, made cooking fires, and prepared to eat. At this opportune time, the English attacked and a large number of Spanish soldiers were killed, wounded, or captured. This became known as the Battle of Bloody Marsh because it was said the marsh was red with the blood of the dead and wounded. In vain the Spanish officers tried to rally their men, but the troops were in such panic and disorder that the commands went unheeded. So, the Spaniards retreated to their camp near Fort St. Simons, and General Oglethorpe collected his forces at Frederica.

Learning of dissension among the Spanish commanders, General Oglethorpe decided to make a night attack upon their main body, hoping that by surprise and their divided opinions, he might drive them from the island. In this, however, he was disappointed. When they were within sight of the enemy camp, one of his soldiers, a Frenchman, deserted to the enemy. Knowing that the deserter would reveal the weakness of his army, he by quick wit found an escape from the threatened danger. Perhaps the ability to devise such quick and clever strategy is the thing which set General James Oglethorpe apart from the ordinary soldier.

He decided to pretend that the deserter was not a deserter at all, but a spy. In order to deceive the Spanish commander, he liberated a prisoner and gave him a sum of money to carry a letter and give it privately to the French deserter. It was written in the French language as if from a friend of his, telling him to make it appear to the Spaniards that Frederica was in a defenseless state. It told him to urge them to attack at once, but if he could not persuade them to attack, he was then to try to persuade them to remain three days longer where they were. By that time British ships of war with two thousand troops would have arrived from South Carolina.

Of course as Oglethorpe hoped, this letter fell into the hands of General Montiano. The Spanish were perplexed over its contents, and the Frenchman put in irons as a double spy. Fortunately, while the council of war was deliberating what course to pursue, three ships did actually come into sight off the bar. The Governor of South Carolina had sent them to survey the situation on the Georgia coast, but were not supposed to land or to fight. Yet the Spanish immediately assumed them to be the ships mentioned in the letter, and in a moment of consternation decided to burn Fort St. Simons, hastily embark, and flee.

The Spanish had no way of knowing that Governor Bull of South Carolina had only sent the ships to see if the Spanish were in control of St. Simons harbor or not, and that they had been ordered to return immediately without engaging in battle. The Spanish commander, not being willing to risk his whole army and fleet at what he thought was an impending battle, put out to sea in retreat.

The success of General Oglethorpe in this campaign was truly wonderful. With a handful of men he had defeated and baffled a well-equipped army and saved Georgia from a formidable invasion. Since the avowed object of the Spanish was to exterminate the English colonies in America, if they had succeeded against Frederica, all the other colonies would have been in danger. For a long time General Oglethorpe expected the return of the enemy, and he strengthened the defenses for this, but the enemy never returned. It was five years later that peace was restored between the contending nations, and the threat was fully eliminated.

So this relatively minor skirmish at Bloody Marsh was a decisive battle for the world as it meant that forever the territory of Georgia and northward would be English; the language, the customs, the traditions English, not Spanish.

In 1743, having completed his task, General Oglethorpe returned to England. After a few years it became obvious that the troops were no longer needed, so they were withdrawn. With the troops gone the town gradually declined until finally it was totally abandoned. Some of the tabby from the walls was hauled away for other construction including the foundation blocks for the lighthouse completed by James Gould in 1811.

The period between the Battle of Bloody Marsh and the great plantation days was a rather uneventful time. Many of the soldiers who had wives and families were given tracts of land; town residents gradually moved to more prosperous places. It was a time of small farms and developing prosperous towns. Only Frederica and Sunbury in Liberty County declined, while other communities prospered. When the Revolutionary War came, many in Georgia saw less reason to break with the home country than those who lived in other places. In fact, many of the more prosperous farmers and merchants remained loyal to the King and moved to the West Indies or Florida or other places to wait out the conflict.

During the Revolutionary War the colony of Georgia suffered very greatly under the Tories and the British. The colony was in a very vulnerable position with little resources. Invasion, occupation, destruction, and disruption of farming brought desperate circumstances and general despair, broken only by the good news of victories of General Nathaniel Greene as he invaded from the north.

Fortunately, things had gone better in the north and after the surrender of Lord Cornwallis, the British Parliament began to listen to the voice of reason, and steps were taken for the establishment of peace. In July 1782 the British army left Savannah, and in the final peace treaty, Georgia was mentioned by name and recognized as a free and independent state.

One other event need be mentioned as of great importance to coastal Georgia. General Nathaniel Greene had been rewarded with a grant of land and a beautiful plantation fourteen miles above Savannah, named Mulberry Grove. Here, after the turmoil of war, he retired with his family to enjoy the delights of a home which he preferred to the one he owned in his native Rhode Island. He died here in 1786, from sunstroke, and was buried on the estate. His widow continued to reside here, and she hired Eli Whitney as a tutor to her children. He often heard Mrs. Greene complain of the tedious process of picking by hand the seed from cotton. Sometimes she would playfully entreat him, as he possessed some mechanical talent, to devise a quicker way to accomplish this disagreeable task. Thus, stimulated, he invented the cotton gin, a machine which immensely increased the cotton industry of the world.

Particularly it made possible the Plantation Period of St. Simons Island and vicinity.

IV. EARLY PLANTATION ERA

Introduction to Plantation Days

The great plantations have taken on a story-book character — picturesque, glamorous, romanticized. Each person has formed in his mind images of these farms, their great houses, and their beautiful social occasions.

St. Simons Island and area had fourteen plantations of note. The stories of them have been well told in many places. In order to make these days as easy to understand as possible and to avoid the confusion of too many details, I am telling the history of the four greatest plantations on St. Simons Island: Hamilton, Retreat, Hampton, and Cannon's Point. The story of these is divided into two sections: the early plantation days, with the development and growth under the original owners; and the plantations in maturity, decline, and demise, under the second and third generations of the families.

During the latter part of the seventeen hundreds, several South Carolina planters came to coastal Georgia. They had already prospered along the Ashley and the Cooper rivers of South Carolina. Yet in those days when rotation of crops and knowledge of fertilizer were hardly known, fields became impoverished so new lands were sought and cleared. Thus, these successful farmers in the older colony looked to the rich alluvial soil of the Altamaha river delta and the coastal islands to the south. They created great plantations and became some of the wealthiest and most influential men of the South, indeed of the entire nation.

The rich lands of the river deltas were ideal for growing rice, planted far enough from the sea for the water to be fresh, as salt water would have damaged the grain, yet near enough that the ebb and flow of the tide could flood the low lying fields.

On St. Simons Island the fields were purchased and cleared and for the most part planted with cotton. They knew immediate prosperity from this crop, not only because of the rich new soil, but some other factors were just right for success:

1) The Spinning Jenny had been invented and introduced in England. With the arrival of the industrial revolution and the building of factories, England was able to make thread and cloth with new and fast machinery.

2) This created an insatiable appetite for cotton to fabricate into cloth to meet a growing demand. So the plantation farmer could market all the cotton he could grow. His agent, called a factor, in a city such as Savannah, shipped directly to the docks in Liverpool.

3) Large production was possible because of the invention of the cotton gin by Eli Whitney, which provided a means of removing the seed before it was put into bales for shipment. So, planters moved here from other areas, bringing their slaves with them, clearing the land, and producing a very profitable crop.

4) Perhaps most important of all to St. Simons Island was the development of a special, fine, long staple cotton, which became known as Sea Island cotton. The planters had experimented with various kinds of cotton. Most of it was of short fibers; some produced good plants, but not much cotton; some produced well, but were not of good color.

In 1786 the seed of a variety of cotton was sent to James Spaulding of Retreat Plantation by a friend, Col. Roger Kelsal, a Loyalist who had refugeed in the Bahamas during the Revolutionary War. This seed had been developed in the West Indies on the island of Anguilla, and for years after its introduction was known as Anguilla cotton. It thrived in Georgia and produced a fine, long staple, much prized in the markets of England. Later it became known as Sea Island cotton and became the staple crop of all the plantations of the coastal area. In good years it brought premium prices. The finest would bring 50¢ a pound in contrast to around 42¢ for that of other kinds. The possible fortunes to be made by the great plantations can be understood by realizing that the fields could have a crop ready for harvest at a value of $100,000 in money of 1820 value!

Of course, we are writing only of these great plantations in their early and most prosperous days. As we will be

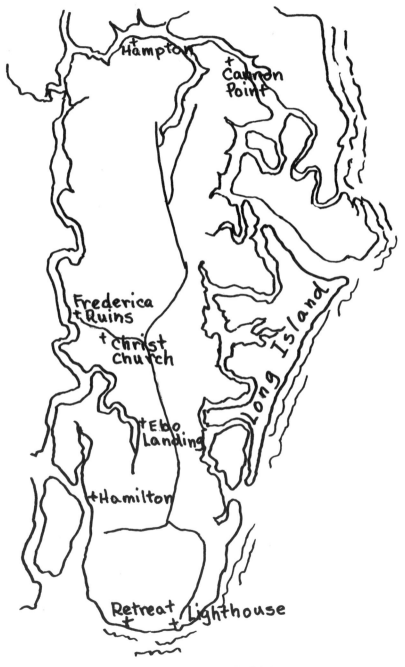

PLANTATION DAYS

seeing later, the price over the plantation period probably averaged about 23¢ a pound. Fields, too, weren't always as productive over the entire period, averaging about 137 pounds of lint cotton per acre, net proceeds per laborer averaging about $83 per year. It should also be remembered that the plantations were almost self-sufficient. They grew their food, raised their animals, fabricated almost everything they needed from boats to hardware. About one-half of the plantation land was used for grain crops to support the plantation.

Hamilton Plantation

Hamilton Plantation was built on the land known as Gascoigne Bluff, and today is where the causeway comes onto the island, including the land of large trees of the county park and the grounds of Epworth-by-the Sea. The first owner of this tract of land was Captain James Gascoigne, commander of the sloop-o-war, Hawk, which convoyed the settlers to Frederica in 1736. As the Captain was in charge of the ships stationed in the area for the defense of the colony, so it was in these waters that the vessels were anchored and kept in repair. So this point might be called Georgia's first naval base. The captain's home soon became known as Gascoigne's Bluff. His plantation here was destroyed by the Spaniards when they invaded St. Simons in 1742. Not long after this, the Captain returned to England to live.

Cotton was cultivated here on this land by Major Alexander Bissett and by Richard Leake during the seventeen-eighties. This was one of the earliest plantings of Sea Island cotton in the United States. Here also, live oak timbers were cut and shipped north to be used in construction of the first ships of the American navy, including the Constitution, known as "Old Ironsides".

In 1793 James Hamilton, with his friend John Couper came to St. Simons Island. Both had come from Scotland, and after being in business together in South Carolina for a few years, purchased land in Georgia. James Hamilton named his land Hamilton Plantation; John Couper continued to call his Cannon's Point, after the first owner in Oglethorpe's day.

Soon this plantation of James Hamilton became one of the richest on the island. The fertile land produced crops of quality cotton which brought premium prices in the London market. The wharf here was the shipping point for the entire south end of the island. He built a two story frame house fronting on the river. It had sturdy colonial lines on high latticed foundations and a wide piazza. Spacious gardens and broad lawns surrounded the plantation house. The fertile land and high cotton prices were so very productive of income that by 1820 Mr. Hamilton was one of the richest men in America. His business enterprises were far flung, and sometimes he traveled to far places of the world. He brought seeds of exotic plants to his friend John Couper who was very interested in horticulture. On one occasion Mr. Hamilton sent a cotton plant from Siam. It grew large, was of a rich purple color, both in foliage and in blossom, but perished without ripening its fruit.

In the early 1820's Mr. Hamilton decided to retire from his active plantation labors and move to Philadelphia. He sold most of his Georgia land except Hamilton Plantation, and built a fine home in Philadelphia, where he lived in great splendor. His plantation had made him one of the richest men in America and one of the country's first millionaires. Looking back, we can now see that he rather wisely liquidated his holdings at about the right time. Did he forsee that soon these great profits in cotton would be in decline? James Hamilton died in Philadelphia in 1829.

Cabin for Household Slaves — Hamilton Plantation

Hampton Plantation

Hampton Plantation or Butler's Point was on the north end of the island. General Oglethorpe had located nineteen soldiers and their families on this bluff in 1738 in keeping with his practice of settling soldiers and some citizens on the various bluffs of the rivers to prevent the Spanish from making a surprise landing on the island. Here on the north end of the island he had started a settlement which he called Newhampton, which soon became just Hampton. After the Battle of Bloody Marsh on July 7, 1742, and the peace treaty of 1748 ending the war of Jenkins' Ear, the regiment disbanded, and soon St. Simons Island was practically deserted.

Later in the century, the land became the property of Major Pierce Butler, who came to Georgia from South Carolina; he built it into one of the great plantations. Major Butler was born in Ireland in 1744. As a major in the British army he came to America in 1766 with the 29th British Regiment. He was first stationed in Boston, but soon moved to Charleston, S.C. Here in 1771 he met and married Polly Middleton, a South Carolina heiress. Resigning his army position, he cast his lot with the colonists and became prominent in the affairs of that state. He was a delegate from South Carolina to the Congress of 1787, served as a member of the Convention that framed the Federal Constitution, and was a United States Senator.

After his wife died in 1790 he began to acquire large land holdings in Georgia, including Hampton Point. He brought most of his slaves to Georgia and built this land into a great cotton plantation. He also owned Butler Island in the Altamaha river, which lowland he surrounded by a dike planted on top with orange trees. Here on this easily flooded land, rice was cultivated. The third plantation he owned was Woodville, a short distance away.

Major Butler was said to be stiff and ceremonious in his manner. As a military man, he was a stern disciplinarian, governing the slaves on his plantation with military strictness. They were not allowed to visit the slaves on the adjoining plantations, not even those in close proximity. He seemed to feel that he could not control his slaves unless he kept them away from outside influences.

Hampton was the only plantation in this section where such conditions existed. The Butler plantations were models of efficiency. Everything needed was manufactured on the plantation from shoes and clothes, to boats, furniture, and tools.

The hospitality of Hampton was dispensed with great formality. The casual visitor arriving by boat had to state his name and business to a warden at the dock before he was escorted to the Butler mansion. Since Major Butler was a prominent figure in the public life of the nation, he entertained many distinguished people on his island estate. His hospitality of Hampton was even extended to business, social, and political friends during the months he was not in residence. Major Butler never considered this as his home. His residence was in Charleston, and later in Philadelphia.

Major Pierce Butler of Hampton Point

Coming here only in the winter months or when his direct supervision was needed, the plantation was put under the management of Roswell King, and later his son, Roswell King, Jr. Together these men ruled the plantation for 36 years for their usually absentee owner.

In 1804 the plantation provided sanctuary for Vice-President Aaron Burr, fugitive from public indignation over the duel in which Alexander Hamilton was killed. Feeling very keenly the criticism, he sought refuge in the South, where dueling was not frowned upon. His old friend, Major Butler, with whom he had served in the Senate of the United States, invited him to visit Butler's Point. Aaron Burr spent several weeks here, and in the absence of Senator Butler, was entertained by residents of St. Simons and of towns on the mainland. He even made a trip down the Inland Waterway to St. Marys to visit an old friend from law school, Major Archibald Clark.

Hampton remained one of the finest and most luxurious places on the island as long as Major Butler used it for a part time home, but after he settled in Philadelphia and left the estate in charge of overseers, there was no longer any reason to operate the plantation on such a lavish scale. It continued to be a very profitable enterprise, but as the years passed the non-essentials were neglected. Maintenance was postponed to allow the showing of large profits, the big house was unoccupied and badly run down, and gardens were overgrown and neglected.

So this plantation, in contrast with those occupied by the owners, developed many of the problems and conditions of absentee ownership and the authority given to hired managers and slave drivers. Major Butler died in 1822.

Cannon's Point

Cannon's Point was the home of the John Couper family. It bordered on the Hampton River at the northeast part of St. Simons Island. Across the marshes and river in the distance was a view of Little St. Simons Island. This plantation was the setting for the magnetic personality of its owner. John Couper was a man of distinction — cultured, charming, witty, a great host. Since he lived until the age of 91, being buried in Christ Church cemetery in 1850, he lived through almost the entire plantation era. The spacious house was built in 1804 to face the river, the English style basement of tabby, with the second and half story above of wood, painted white with green shutters. A Sago palm hedge surrounded the house on all but the river side. Being an innovator, with an interest in agricultural experimentation, he was soon surrounded with exotic plants from all over the world, as well as olive groves, orange and lemon trees, date palms bearing fruit, and of course fields of cotton, which would bring many thousand dollars for the crop.

John Couper was born in Scotland, near Glasgow, the son of a Presbyterian minister. When he was only sixteen years of age, he persuaded his father to allow him to join other young men who were coming to the colonies. Thus in 1775, he arrived in Georgia as an apprentice to the Savannah branch of an English business firm. Later he went into business in Sunbury where he became a prosperous merchant. In partnership with James Hamilton several tracts of land were purchased on St. Simons Island. Being already a successful business man, he wanted to turn his talents to horticulture, and sensing the possibilities of the soil of the coastal islands to produce a great variety of plants, he and his wife decided to move to St. Simons Island. So in 1792 they selected a homesite at Cannon's Point and began building a remarkable plantation. His friend James Hamilton settled at Gascoigne Bluff at about the same time. Hamilton's business interests took him to the far corners of the world, thus he was able to send seeds and plants of all kinds to John Couper for experimentation on the St. Simons plantation.

Plantation House — Cannon's Point (drawing from a photograph of an oil painting)

In the gardens here every fruit and flower, every shrub and tree that could be induced to thrive in its surroundings, could be found. President Thomas Jefferson was interested in experimenting with the cultivation of olives in the United States, so he induced John Couper to order some olive trees from Marseilles. The grove of 200 trees did well and yielded a fine quality of oil from its fruit.

John Couper had many other interests in addition to agriculture. He served in the state legislature; was a member of the convention to draw up the state constitution; and was active in Christ Church and various community organizations.

The timbers for the building of the Constitution, better known as Old Ironsides, were cut on St. Simons Island, loaded at Gascoigne Bluff, and carried by boat to Boston, where the vessel was built and launched in 1797. The first tree felled for the Constitution was an immense live oak at Cannon's Point, whose size and shape made it desirable for use as the stern-post. It was said that the stump of this tree was banded with an iron band bearing the inscription "U.S. Frigate Constitution, 1794". This stump was carried to the International Cotton Exposition held in Atlanta in 1895 (or was it 1881, as some report?); and was not returned to St. Simons Island.

Mr. Couper gave the land to the government for the first lighthouse, to be built on the south end of the island, deeding four acres in 1804. The lighthouse was completed in 1811 by James Gould. It was octagonal, 75 feet tall, and constructed of tabby. The foundation was made of blocks of very old, hard tabby, cut from the ruins of old Ft. Frederica. It tapered from a 25 foot base to 10 feet at the top. An iron lamp equipped with oil lamps was suspended by chains. The upper division of 12½ feet was constructed of the "best northern brick", as local brick were soft, and contained too much sand.

Cannon's Point plantation was a place where a constant stream of guests were welcome. Men from all over the world came to visit and to see for themselves the fruits of the horticultural experimentations. Visitors were enchanted by John Couper himself. His ready wit, his conversations, his knowledge of the world at large, plus his polite and friendly manner made him seem a true representative of the southern gentleman. Even Fanny

Kemble, who was so critical of the South and most of the people she found there in 1839, saw charm and principles in John Couper, which she failed to see in anyone else in the area.

So it was that Cannon's Point Plantation, with cotton as its great crop and presided over by a southern gentleman, seems to have taken on an excellent way of life. Broad verandahs, beautiful gardens, dignity of manner and dress, gracious entertaining gives it almost a storybook image.

Retreat Plantation

Retreat Plantation was at the south end of the island. In 1736 General Oglethorpe stationed John Humble on this land and appointed him first pilot for this harbor. His home stood about where the Sea Island Golf Club now stands. Later these lands were granted to John Clubb as bounty for his service in Oglethorpe's Regiment. Clubb lived here until 1786 when he sold it to Thomas Spaulding from Scotland. That same year Mr. Spaulding received seed of a variety of cotton from a friend who was a Loyalist and had refugeed in the Bahamas during the Revolution. Developed in the Island of Anguilla in the West Indies, it was first known as Anguilla cotton, then later as Sea Island cotton. It was especially prized and brought a premium price in England.

After living here a few years, Mr. Spaulding decided to purchase Sapelo Island. So, he sold Retreat Plantation to Major William Page and his wife Hannah.

Major Page had come to the island to visit his friend, Major Pierce Butler of Butler Point. During the visit here their young child, Ann Matilda Page, grew healthy. They were overjoyed about this, for all of their earlier children had died, and they much wanted this child to be well and strong. So encouraged by this improvement in health, they decided to make St. Simons Island their home.

Purchasing Retreat Plantation, they proceeded to build it into one of the greatest cotton plantations in the South. The simple frame house was of sturdy English design. It faced the beach, the sound, and Jekyll Island beyond. Sea Island cotton was cultivated, and was of such fine quality that it brought 50¢ a pound in contrast to about 42¢ for other cotton grown on the island. Being one of the wealthiest men in the South, Major Page had many interests which required much travel, even weeks at a time. No matter though, the baby, now grown into a talented young woman, quickly learned the skills of management of her father. Ann Matilda operated the plantation with great skill during the times her father was away. As the plantation prospered under her leadership, the house was enlarged and other buildings were built.

Ann Matilda was a very popular young woman and much sought after by the young men of the South. It proved to be Thomas Butler King of Massachusetts who won her. He had come south to visit his brother, then remained to practice law. They were married in December 1824. Only two years later Ann's parents died and she inherited Retreat Plantation and other vast holdings. So automatically her husband became one of the wealthiest planters of the Georgia coast.

Thomas Butler King, an attorney, became involved in public affairs and politics. His wife continued to run the plantation. Mr. King was elected to the Georgia Senate; then to the United States Congress. In Washington Mr. King sponsored the bill that established a navy. Great honors came to him in political life. In 1851-52 he served as Collector of the Port of San Francisco; he promoted the construction of a transcontinental railroad; promoted a gold mining company.

Meanwhile, his wife continued to run a very profitable plantation, one in which the storybook image of the plantation was almost a reality.

An Unusual Society

In the first quarter of the nineteenth century we find on St. Simons Island a society which was a melange of Old World courtesy and refinement. The early planters of the Georgia coast were men of education, culture, and broad experience. Here were the son of a great English family, Major Butler; a gentleman of Scotch birth, Mr. John Couper; an Oxford graduate, Mr. George Baillie; an officer of the Revolution, Major Page; and a number of officers of the British army, such as Captain Alexander Wylly, Lt. Col. Wardrobe, who had served with Napier and Wellington in India, Dr. William Fraser, who had been surgeon in chief to the East India forces and for many years resided in Calcutta.

These men are those who helped in the building of Georgia. John Couper had known it in pre-Revolutionary days, and the leaders in this struggle were his familiar friends. Major Page had met and known the men who had ruled the councils of the provincial government. Poulain du Bignon of Jekyll had witnessed the splendor of the Mogul Empire in India, and had seen and helped it crumble before British arms.

When these men gathered together, their talk was not always of crops and the need of rain, but of battles, seiges, and great events of history. Yet in this society there was also an air of democratic simplicity. They did not display evidence of great wealth, but everywhere there was immense comfort and unbounded hospitality. To be a guest of one family was to be a welcome guest to all. The tables were spread abundantly with home grown produce, glasses filled with foreign wine and brandy, food often prepared by accomplished chefs.

In 1820 Major Butler, although he had himself left the island five years earlier, purchased the St. Clair house and gave it, for a nominal rent, to a club formed by the planters of St. Simons. It was to be used solely for their social pleasure, and they called it the St. Clair Club. Monthly dinners were given, each member in rotation furnishing the dinner, service, and the wines. Three outside guests were allowed to be invited, and these often came from as far away as Savannah, St. Mary's, and Augusta. These were occasions of extraordinary conviviality — elegant dining, song, and story.

The elegance of such a dinner party is described by Charles Wylly for the night of December 7, 1821. We are not sure of the source of his information for a party fifteen years before his birth, but the specific date and details must have come from his father who was present, or else some documents at hand which described it. (This is included in the book of Charles Wylly, **These Memories, 1916.**)

The date is December 7, 1821. The hour is 5:00 p.m. The slanting rays of the sun crimson the green lawn and light the festoons of moss draping the old oaks that shade the house. Most magnificent of these is ''Old England'', which no other could compare for size or girth or spread of limb.

Inside, the dining room is made cheerful by the glow of a great wood fire. The table, with places for fourteen, is covered with the snowiest of damasks, and lit by a score of candles, made from the wax of the myrtle berry that covers the salt marshes, and placed in brass candlesticks that are polished like gold. The dishes are of blue East India china.

The host on this occasion is evidently Mr. John Couper, for the cook is the immortal Sans Foix, and the waiters are Sandy, Johnny, and Old Dick from Cannon's Point, assisted by James Dennison from the Village. Since nine o'clock in the morning they have been busy in the kitchen, and now at five o'clock, all is in readiness.

The guests are arriving — no one, whatever his age, is so effeminate as to use carriage or chaise — are mounted on wiry steeds, whose living has been drawn from marsh moss and shucks, but who show in gait and mettle their descent from Spanish and Arab stock. Each one is accompanied by one or two lack boys, eager for the fragments of the feast.

The Club members present on this occasion were: John Couper, John Fraser, Dr. William Fraser, Alexander Wylly, his son Alexander William Wylly, William Page, Raymond Demere, George Baillie, Benjamin Cater, William Armstrong, and Daniel Heyward Brailsford. The three outside guests of the club were: Captain Du Bignon of Jekyll Island, Dr. James Troup of Darien, and Mr. Thomas Charlton of Savannah.

Dinners at that time on the coast were not served in courses, excepting the soup and dessert, everything else being placed on the table at once, and usually kept hot under highly polished covers of Britannia ware. Mr. James Hamilton had his covers made of silver, and left them by will to his daughter, Isabella Corbin de Dampiere.

This night the guests seated themselves around the table, and the dinner was served. Two soups: one a clam broth, the other a chicken mulligatawny, were served first. Then fish, shrimp pies, crab in shell, roasts, and vegetables were placed in one service. The dessert was simple — tartlets of orange marmalade, dried fruits, and nuts.

The dishes were disposed of and the table cloth removed, amid general gossip and talk among the guests.

Then the great punch bowl was brought in, with its mixture of rum, brandy, sugar, lemon juice, and peel. The wine glasses were pushed aside, and stubby bottle-shaped glass mugs were handed around. The chairman of the meeting arises, and announces that "the health of the President of the United States would be drank, standing and with cheers." Mr. Charlton, responding, said the thanks of the whole country were due President Monroe for his wise conduct of affairs. After this opening of the evening there is much filling of mugs, nodding of heads one to another, with words of good wishes — "Happy Days to You," and the like. Songs are called for, and Captain Du Bignon in a husky voice gives, "Cheer up, my lads, Cheer up!". Captain John Fraser follows in a fine tenor with "A Valiant Soldier I Dare To Name," which is received with much applause. Dr. William Fraser is called upon for his Hindu song, a translation of which is:

Songster sweet, begin the lay,
Always fresh and ever gay.
Bring me quick inspiring wine,
Always fresh and ever fine.

To this song fiddler Johnny adds an accompaniment, with admiration on his glowing face.

The entire purpose of these dinners is not the mere enjoyment of eating and drinking, for there is much interesting conversation. George Baillie, who talks with knowledge and spirit on almost every subject, has been discussing Sheridan and Moliere with his uncle, Captain Wylly, who observes, "Wit is only what every one would have said, could he have thought of it". "Yes, dear Uncle," answers George, "Call in a good surgeon, and even yourself might be delivered of it".

Dr. Troup had been recounting to Major Page the incidents of his visit to an Indian cousin in the Alabama Creek Territory. He had visited that remarkable man, Alexander McGillivray, the virtual emperor of the Creeks, at Broken Arrow in the Coosa Valley. He tells of the beauty and fertility of the lands on the banks of the Coosa and Tallapoosa, and of the Indian villages with their comfortable log cabins, gardens, and fields.

Dr. Fraser has been telling old Raymond Demere of the Mogul empire where diamonds, rubies, and pearls are the loot of the common solider, and the eyes of the miserly man sparkle with covetousness.

Two hours pass in this pleasant way, when the chairman rises, raps smartly on the table for silence and says "Gentlemen, I propose the joint health of our esteemed friends, Mr. and Mrs. John Couper, and that of the baby boy presented by Mrs. Couper for the admiration of its father and every resident on the island — William Audley Couper. Waiter, fill every glass." The toast is drunk enthusiastically.

Mr. Couper lifts his massive frame and stands erect. Then, clearing his throat, he says, "I thank you my friends for this honor. I should respond with song, but the condition of my throat forbids," and he then continues with an amusing anecdote that sets the table roaring, while his fiddler Johnny works frantically on his bow.

Punch is ordered served all around, servants included, these imbibing their drinks in corners and hallways and wishing that club dinners were everyday occurrences.

Nine strikes of the clock, and "Auld Lang Syne" is sung as all stand with joined hands. The horses are called for, and Captain Wylly and Major Page are the first to say good-night. Attended by their faithful body servants, James Dennison and old Neptune, they ride away to the south. The others follow, each with a black man as friend and servant, to ride behind if necessary to help the brave souls back to the forgiveness of home. But in truth, aid was not often needed.

Christ Church was also a center of social life. The Sunday worship at 11:00 was well attended. However, people began to arrive soon after nine o'clock for a time of visiting and gossip. The men on arriving seated themselves outside on benches under the trees, and receiving their mail, which was brought to the church by the postmaster. They read their letters, discussed the latest news from Washington, or Savannah, or Milledgeville or most anywhere, until it was time for the worship.

Most of the men also belonged to the Agricultural and Sporting Club. This group often joined in activities with the Camden Hunt Club on the mainland. These members met and hunted twice a month, the game consisting of deer, pigs, cows, bulls, wildcats, and turkeys.

So, this was the good life of the Georgia Coast in the

early plantation days. Having the same interests and the same problems to solve, they enjoyed this close-knit society where they could share their experiences and exchange ideas. Outweighing any excesses and faults, their great generosity of heart, great honesty of purpose, and unblemished integrity mark their leadership of this unique era.

FANNY KEMBLE, a famous English actress, was married to Pierce Butler owner of Hampton plantation. Her visit to the plantation in 1839 resulted in a condemnation of slavery as she saw it. She is portrayed during this visit showing a St. Simons scene through the window behind her.

V. PLANTATIONS IN MATURITY AND DECLINE

By the late 1820's the second generation was taking over the ownership and management of the plantations. The great men who developed the plantations in the 1790's were getting older. They had made great success as planters and business men. Now it was time for a more splendid life in the city, or was time to give the problems of farm management to their sons.

So, sometime around 1825 to 1835, the early plantation era came to an end; and the continuing history of the plantations is a distinct period. Of course, these great plantations continued in maturity. In fact their well developed organization, the storybook social life, the outward prosperity, seemed to continue for a long time. However, by this time the forces of decay had already begun. Several things contributed to this.

1. The soil was not as fertile and productive as in earlier years. The rotation of crops and fertilizers were not well known or as much used as today we know them to be.

2. Recession in England, and other factors there, caused a dramatic decline in the demand and the price of cotton. The price fell to less than one-half of what it had been in earlier years.

3. There was increasing controversy about the use of slaves. This put pressure upon the owners and managers of the plantations who were so dependant on hand labor to produce the crops. The importation of new slaves from Africa was prohibited in Georgia. Then actually quite a smuggling trade in slaves came to exist. Boats could hide their cargos in the rivers and inlets of the island until the slaves could be sold and transported elsewhere.

As an interesting footnote: Ebo Landing on Dunbar Creek was one of the best of these shelters. Tradition says that a group of Negroes from the Ebo tribe in Africa were being held here until they could be shipped to the slave markets elsewhere. Included among them was the very proud chief of this tribe. Seeing nothing ahead but a very miserable future, they all walked into the water and drowned themselves rather than be slaves, saying "The water brought us here; the water will take us away."

4. Absentee ownership in the second and third generation often brought less interested management, allowed the buildings to run down, and brought excesses in the treatment of the slaves.

Thus, even in the years before the War Between the States, the plantation system was already past its prime. Then the whirlwind of war almost completely destroyed it. Later post-war efforts for revival proved discouraging and were for the most part unsuccessful.

In this chapter we are describing the same four plantations and what happened to them in maturity and decline.

Hamilton Plantation — later days

At the death of James Hamilton in 1829, this plantation and other land was inherited by his only daughter, Agnes Rebecca Hamilton, who was married to Francis P. Corbin. The Corbins lived in Paris, France with their three children — Constance (who married a French nobleman); Isabella, and Richard. The will of James Hamilton appointed his namesake and son of his friend John Couper, James Hamilton Couper as the administrator of the estate and as a trustee to manage it until the youngest grandchild Richard became of age.

Captain John Fraser and his wife Ann Couper were secured to manage the operation of the farm and live in the Hamilton Plantation house. The Captain retired from the British navy to accept this position. Mrs. Fraser was a sister of James Hamilton Couper, the trustee of the estate. The beautiful Ann had a flair for entertaining; so these days there with her children was probably the happiest time of all the Hamilton Plantation era. The plantation seemed to prosper, and it took on a storybook atmosphere. Fanny Kemble Butler, who was entertained there in 1839, saw the simple colonial house with shuttered front verandah and high latticed foundations surrounded by a hedge of flowering yucca. She viewed the wide lawns sloping down to the banks of the Frederica river; the shell walks leading through formal gardens to the rose garden, to the cutting garden, to the herb garden, all divided by picket fences and boxwood hedges. She described it as "By far the finest place on the island."

Years later, the management went to William Audley Couper, brother of Ann. It was during this period that in 1852 a great tragedy occurred. The Magnolia, a side-wheeled steamboat that traveled the Inland Waterway, had just cleared the wharf at Hamilton with a cargo of passengers and cotton when the boiler exploded. Many were killed and others terribly burned and maimed. The second floor of the large tabby barn was converted to a hospital; bales of cotton were cut open to make beds. Many of the victims remained here for weeks before they were able to leave. The family today still treasures a handsome engraved silver pitcher, gift from the grateful survivors of the Magnolia.

Around this time, James Hamilton Couper — now a prosperous planter living at "Hopeton on the Altamaha" — purchased Hamilton Plantation from the Corbin children who still lived in Paris. Interestingly, the Corbins always considered themselves Georgians, although they lived in France. In fact, during the War Between the States, the grandson Richard W. Corbin slipped into Wilmington, N.C. on a blockade runner, made his way to Virginia and served as an Aide on General Fields's staff of General Longstreet's Corps. After the war he returned to France feeling he had done his duty.

Of course, the Civil War effectively destroyed the plantations on the island. With the plantation despoiled, the slaves freed, and a lien on the land for $80,000 from a note incurred three years before the war, James Hamilton Couper had to give it up. The property was taken for debt by Richard Corbin of Paris, from whom he had purchased the plantation several years before.

As with the other plantations, Hamilton Plantation could not grow cotton without the hand labor of slaves, so for many years it grew up in brush as the wilderness took over again.

Yet the land still had much further use, as we shall describe in later periods of its history.

Hampton Plantation — later days

When Major Pierce Butler died in Philadelphia in 1822, he willed Hampton Point and his other Georgia plantations (Butler Island and Woodville) to his two grandsons — John and Pierce. They were children of his daughter Sarah who had married a Philadelphia doctor, Dr. John Mease. The will, however, stipulated that in order to inherit the land the grandsons would have to assume the family name of Butler. Thus, they changed their names from Mease to Butler in order to qualify for the inheritance. Income was provided for his unmarried daughter, Frances, who also with Roswell King (the manager of Hampton) were to be co-administrators of the estate. Frances died in 1836.

Great notoriety came to this plantation because of the visit here in 1839 of Fanny Kemble Butler and the diary which she kept. "Fanny" (Frances Anne Kemble) was an English actress of remarkable talents. Besides being an actress and dramatic reader, she was a writer of prose and poetry. She came from a family of fine actors. Her debut

Fanny Kemble

Pierce Mease Butler

on the stage was made in London in 1829 as Juliet. Her success was immediate. In 1832 she toured the principal cities of America where she met equal success. Society welcomed her with open arms and she met most of the important men and women of America.

A handsome, wealthy, young socialite pursued her from city to city admiring her beauty and talent. In 1834 this Pierce Butler, the grandson of Major Pierce Butler of St. Simons Island persuaded her to marry him. The Butler mansion in Philadelphia was an elegant establishment, perhaps the finest in the city, a setting for their amiable social life.

Apparently, as a young girl in her early twenties, it had not occurred to Fanny to wonder about the source of her husband's wealth and income. It wasn't until after her marriage did it dawn on her that all of this wealth and splendor they had to enjoy was the result of the labor of slaves on plantations in far away Georgia. She was horrified everytime she thought of this splendid life of hers coming from over 700 slaves which they owned! She had grown up in England where the abolitionist movement had been in existence for fifty years and was about to reach its climax. The young girl Fanny had no particular relationship to this abolitionist movement, but by association it had ingrained in her some strong feelings against slavery.

Wanting to see the plantations and its slaves for herself, and perhaps thinking she could persuade her husband to free his slaves, she asked to make a trip to Georgia. Her husband and his co-owner brother were not much in favor of this trip, but she persisted. So in December of 1838, Pierce Butler and his wife and two children, Sally age three and Fanny age seven months, made the trip. (The account of this trip from Philadelphia to Darien, Georgia is very interesting, and is found in the opening chapters of her "Journal of a Residence on a Georgia Plantation", although this part was not printed in the original editions.)

She lived for a few months on Butler Island rice plantation; then moved to Hampton Point for another few weeks stay. Each day she kept a Journal of her activities and impressions. Daily she enjoyed the natural beauty of the area; interviewed various slaves who often came to her for some need; observed how life and work proceeded

*The house where Fanny Kemble lived while visiting the plantations
in Georgia in 1839.*

on the plantations. Generally she was horrified at what she
saw and found, and was very critical of many of the
people she met.

The Butlers returned to Philadelphia after a few
months, and because of her attitude the family refused to
allow her to come again when she wanted to make a later
trip.

Her marriage, apparently an unhappy one for many
other reasons besides slavery, did not last. Bitterness
developed between them, and in 1846 she moved from the
home. Divorce followed two years later. She lived in
Lenox, Massachusetts until 1856 when she returned to
England.

All of this time her Journal from Georgia lay unread,

except by some close friends. However, during the War between the North and the South, she was disturbed by the amount of friendly sentiment in England toward the South. Many newspapers played down the evils of slavery. There was real sentiment to break the blockade of southern ports, which might mean war with the United States. There was much favor in granting a loan to the Confederate States to help them finance the war.

To forestall these things, Fanny Kemble decided to publish her "Journal of a Residence on a Georgia Plantation, 1838-39". This publication in 1863 was almost a quarter century after it was written. By this time, not only had her marriage been long broken, but the plantations written about were no longer in existence! The panic of 1857 had caused Pierce Butler to sell out. His slaves had been auctioned in Savannah where the 429 men, women, and children brought $303,850.00, or an average of more than $708 a head. The slaves were sold off in family groups of two to seven persons each.

The publication of her Journal caused a sensation. Perhaps it was the thing that turned the tide of public opinion against the South. The loan was not made, a fact which helped materially in deciding the fate of the Confederacy.

As was true with most plantations, the war brought the demise of Hampton Plantation. Some effort was made to revive it on a share-crop basis, but without success. The old mansion burned in 1871; the owners had completely given up the planting of cotton.

So the land lay unoccupied, and the property gradually returned to the wilderness from which it came. Since then, time has completed its cycle. During World War II there was a lookout on the lonely northwest tip of St. Simons where Oglethorpe had stationed his Newhampton outpost two centuries before. Even now, the land is being platted into building lots to again serve as homes for those from the north, beckoned to the island by its beauty, history, and gentle weather.

Cannon's Point — later days

Cannon's Point in its maturity and early decline continued to be dominated by the extraordinary personality of John Couper since he lived to be 91 years of age. Men from all over the world came to visit and see for themselves the fruits of his horticultural experiments. His wife Rebecca was an accomplished housewife and charming hostess. Fine food and perfect service at their table was known far and wide. Their cook, Sans Foix, was truly the best chef in his profession; his French dishes captivated the taste of John Couper and his guests. With the finest of seafood at the door, the great variety of fruits and vegetables from their orchards and gardens, the fowls and meats, it was nearly always a feast at the Couper table. There were formal dinners and balls with the ladies in silk and lace and velvet. Visitors were enchanted with John Couper, his ready wit and conversation, his knowledge of science and of the world at large.

But good things come to an end, and the decline in plantation life had already begun. Earlier hurricanes raging on the very exposed location of his land in 1804 and 1824, plus the loss of slaves by enemy seizure in the War of 1812, plus a plague of caterpillars in 1825, plus a drop in cotton prices, had already forced the sale of much of his coastal property in Georgia. By selling these other holdings however, he was able to solve his financial problems. So the Coupers were able to retain their beloved Cannon's Point, where they lived happily past their golden wedding anniversary. After his wife's death in 1845, John Couper spent his remaining years with his eldest son's family at Hopeton Plantation on the mainland. He lived to age 91, passing away in 1850 with burial in Christ Church cemetery. The eldest son, James Hamilton Couper, a very distinguished planter, continued to manage Cannon's Point plantation and used the house as a summer home.

The war came and destroyed this way of life. The land was rented to various tenants after the war, but with little success at cultivation of this once very productive land. The house untenanted, the fields and gardens overgrown, the old times became only memories. Cannon's Point eventually passed into other hands and some of the fields were cultivated to some extent. It is related that the olive trees were still bearing late in the century, and that oil made from them was exhibited in Atlanta at the Exposition of 1898. It is also said that the remaining part of the old Constitution (Old Ironsides) stump was sent to

Atlanta to be displayed and was not returned.

The Cannon's Point house burned near the turn of the century, leaving only the kitchen fireplace, chimney, and crumbling foundations. The land had several different owners, presently the Sea Island Corporation, but has grown up in a tangle of undergrowth, closed to the public, awaiting future development.

Retreat Plantation — later days

This plantation in its maturity continued to be run by Mrs. Thomas Butler King. Her husband was in Washington much of the time. His honors and power in public life increased. In 1851-52 he served as Collector of the Port of San Francisco. In business he promoted a transcontinental railroad, a gold mining company, etc.

In 1836 Loammi Baldwin, an engineer who had worked on the Bunker Hill monument and the dry docks at Charleston, Massachusetts, and Norfolk, Virginia, was here surveying for a railroad. Mr. King asked him to lay out a drainage ditch for Retreat. It was dug in 1836 by slave labor, and it can still be seen today serving its purpose.

Tabby ruins of Slave Hospital — Retreat Plantation

Ann Matilda had laid out New Fields to the north of the plantation, where the airport is now located. In the winter of 1848-49 a new road was built to these New Fields. Permission was obtained to use the slaves for this during the slow season, for it was usually required that the slaves work on public roads at this time of year. The labor required for this project was very great as there were low places to be filled up and there was a continuing mass of palmetto roots to cut through. Trees were set out along the road — 500 trees. This beautiful avenue of live oak trees (Quercus verens) was wide enough for carriages. Today one section remains, with a paved road on either side of the avenue of trees, with the old plantation road in the middle remaining as it was.

The old slave cabin (at the northwest corner of the airport) was one of eight cabins which stood in a row. One was across the road to the north, and six were south of this building. It contained four rooms on the main floor and an attic which was used for sleeping quarters. With center chimney and fireplaces on either side, it could have been for two families, as the attic divided and had two stairs. These were the cabins on what was known as "New Field". Floyd White was born in this house and the last Negro to live there. His mother was a slave of Retreat and his father, Jupiter, belonged to the Postells of Kelvin Grove.

Ruins may still be seen of the ten room slave hospital. The ground floor was used for men; the second floor for women; the third floor attic by the two nurses who lived there. Rooms were 12 x 15 feet, each room having a fireplace and two windows. The staircase was in a wide hall in the center of the house. Careful records were kept. For example, they showed that in 1856 twenty-eight children and two adults had measles and five of the infants died.

The present Sea Island Golf Club was formerly the corn barn of Retreat Plantation. Horse stables were on the ground floor and corn and fodder stored above. Nearby had stood a four story cotton barn, built in 1842. It had the most modern gins of the day. In the ten years between the old lighthouse being destroyed and the present one being constructed, sailors used this cotton barn as a landmark.

In the 1850's the plantation era was coming to an end, and already the shadows of war were closing in. Butler, the eldest son died in 1859, and a few months later Ann Matilda King died. During the war, the son Lord King went into the Confederate Army, accompanied by his body servant Neptune Small. Lord was shot and killed at the Battle of Fredericksburg. In the midst of battle, Neptune made his way to the battlefield, found the body of his master, shouldered it from the field, and somehow managed to get it back to St. Simons Island, where it was buried in the church yard at Christ Church, Frederica. The grave of Neptune Small may be seen in the little burial ground on Retreat Plantation, nearby the present Sea Island Clubhouse.

The Old Clock from Retreat Plantation
During the War Between the States, the gunboat Ethan Allen from the north, stood off St. Simons Island in January, 1863. Sailors made raids against Retreat

Ruins of Plantation House at Retreat

Plantation and carried off the valuables from the house. This included a mantle clock, which was wrapped in a black shawl and taken back to the boat. Soon thereafter, the ship returned to Boston.

Sixty-seven years passed, until in 1930 the clock and shawl were sold at an auction in Attleboro, Massachusetts, in the closing out of an estate. In making repairs to the clock, Edmond H. Gingrass, a collector of antiques, discovered a slip of paper pasted on the back of the dial which read:

"This clock was taken from the Thomas Butler King Plantation on St. Simons Island, Georgia, January 10, 1863, by members of the crew of the United States gunboat, Ethan Allen."

Mr. Gingrass turned the clock over to the local G.A.R. who made contact in Brunswick, Georgia, to see if any remaining members of that family were living to which the clock could be returned. Of course there were such relatives, so a great ceremony was planned for its return after 67 years.

Politicians from both north and south gathered, along with hundreds of other people for the presentation on May 6, 1930. The shawl, also sold at auction, had been purchased by Mr. Warren E. Christie, Foxboro, Mass. He was contacted and returned the shawl in memory of his father, a Union soldier.

The ceremony was held in the only remaining building on Retreat Plantation, the old slave hospital. (It was then the caddies' clubhouse). Rep. John W. Martin, Jr. of Massachusetts presented the clock to Isaac Aiken, a grandson of Thomas King. Senator George of Georgia made an acceptance speech. During the ceremony the old clock ticked away the minutes as it had done there so many years before. The shawl was presented by Congressman Martin to the youngest granddaughter, Mrs. Burford King Aiken, who made a short reply of acceptance. Later a banquet was held to honor the citizens of Attleboro who returned the clock and shawl.

The clock was kept in the clubhouse at the Sea Island Golf Club and was a conversation piece, until alas, the clubhouse burned down in 1935, and the clock was destroyed. The clubhouse could and was rebuilt, but the historic clock had been destroyed forever. The shawl was not on display with the clock in the clubhouse, and although its whereabouts are presently unknown, your author believes that it would not have been discarded, and hopefully might be found and again put on public display.

In 1905 the plantation house was destroyed by fire, and now only the fireplace and some of the foundation remains. Retreat Plantation remained in the possession of the King family until 1926, when it was purchased by the Sea Island Company for a golf course and resort.

The Demise of an Era

So, the storybook life of the plantations was snuffed out by the whirlwind of War Between the States. The old way of life was no longer possible. Cotton prices were low, and the cultivation of rice was too complicated to be profitable in post-war labor conditions. Truthfully, the hand labor involved in large scale production from cotton and rice farming was not possible without slaves. Helplessly, the planters saw the disintegration of the very fabric of their lives. Many of the owners, who were the grandsons of the original planters, regretfully left their ancestral estates and went to the cities where they made connections with the shipping, lumber, and cotton businesses for which their experience had best fitted them. Others who returned to their homes and repaired their fields gradually gave up the struggle. What cultivation of rice had been continued was largely abandoned after a high tide accompanying the hurricane of 1898 broke through the dikes and flooded the marshlands to a depth of nine feet. Later it came to a complete end as the rice land would not support the weight of heavy machinery of mechanized farming. So, the rice fields reverted to marshes, which still fertile, is so important in the food chain of marine life.

NEPTUNE SMALL was the servant of Lord King of Retreat plantation. After the battle of Fredericksburg Neptune carried the body of his fallen master home for burial on St. Simons Island. The land in the pier area was named Neptune park in his honor. Mary Green has painted Neptune from a photograph taken in his later years. The plantation, the soldiers, the grave at Christ Church, and the present Neptune park are all shown.

VI. OLD MILL DAYS 1874—1908

Following the Civil War, life was very difficult on these coastal islands. The plantation owners had suffered financially. The Negroes had been freed, but had no money to buy food and supplies. On St. Simons Island some of the owners gave many of their former slaves land upon which to build a simple cabin and plant gardens. For a while the government sent ships to the beach with food.

Fortunately, a new economic era began when New York financial interests decided to build a lumber mill on St. Simons Island. This brought a change in style of life here. New jobs were created as lumber mills and other buildings were built. Logs were rafted in, and ships came to new wharfs in large numbers to ship the finished lumber to various parts of the world.

In 1868, A.G.P. Dodge and other wealthy New York merchants saw a great profit in southern lumber and organized the Georgia Land and Lumber Company. They purchased large tracts of land and erected mills, and by 1874 had decided upon St. Simons Island as the center of their operation. Gascoigne Bluff and Hamilton Plantation on the Frederica river were purchased. In time there were four mills erected on the property, along with the buildings of the needed supporting community. Logs were floated on rafts from the interior by way of the Satilla and Altamaha rivers and their tributaries. There was a large holding basin into which they were floated until they could be processed. There was a large sawmill, a cypress mill, a planing mill, and one they called the lower mill. There were wharfs on the river for the ships which took the finished product to many parts of the world.

To support this operation many related buildings were needed. There were an office, a boarding house, a church, a school, and various homes. Mr. Anson Dodge, Sr. built a fine home for himself which was named Rose Cottage. This was later occupied by the superintendent of the mills, Warren A. Fuller. Thousands of roses of all kinds and colors surrounded the beautiful Victorian house. It was destroyed by fire in 1884.

St. James Union Church was built in 1880, serving the worship needs of the community until after the mill days came to an end. (In the 1920's the building was deconsecrated and used for a social hall; then in the 1950's was reconsecrated by the Methodists and renamed Lovely Lane Chapel. Today it remains a chapel, without a congregation, open occasionally for weddings and worship. On December 7, 1980, a 100th Anniversary service was held here, the sermon being delivered by Dr.

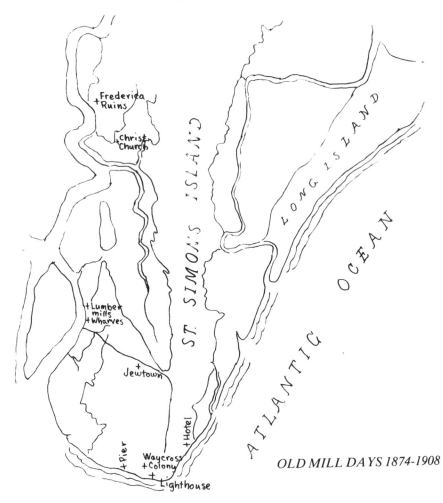

OLD MILL DAYS 1874-1908

Lower Mill

George E. Clary, Sr., long time pastor and leader of the South Georgia Conference of the United Methodist Church.)

Mallon school was built in 1882. The plantation barn became the general store. Its wall may still be seen as part of the new Epworth dining room building. Some of the slave residences are still in existence, which were used for various other purposes during the lumbering days.

There was a great need for fresh water, so it was an important occasion when the first artesian well was drilled in 1885. They found a flow of water of 200 gallons per minute through a six inch pipe at a depth of 437 feet. The well was located in the lumber yard between the large mill and the planing mill. Water rose in a stand pipe 38 feet above the ground and was allowed to flow into a reservoir as high as the top of the mill. From here it was conducted into both of the mill buildings with a force sufficient to throw a stream to any part of either building in case of fire, and without the need of pumps. It also supplied water through pipes to the wharfs to supply the ships with fresh water, as well as to the various buildings of the mills. By this time the mills already had electric lights, elevated railways, and neat well-planned grounds.

Here was probably the largest establishment of its kind in the South. Besides owning 300,000 acres of pine land near Eastman, it made purchases of timber constantly from Darien and various points inland. A newspaper clipping reports at that time (not dated) the mill had on hand awaiting shipment no less than four million feet of merchantable lumber being shipped to coastwise ports and South America as rapidly as it could be loaded. The existing capacity of the mills was then about 125,000 feet per day. Sometimes no less than nine ships were at the wharf awaiting cargo. The mills were a major employer of the island. In 1885 a laborer was paid $1.00 a day for 11½ hours of work. The population around the mills was about 300.

A little settlement down the road east from the mills developed when two merchants from Brunswick, Sig and Robert Levison, built a general store there. The mills, of course, had a commissary or company store, so this general store of the Levison's was set up in competition. The store owners tried to call their settlement Levisonton, but people found this name to be a tongue-twister and instead started to refer to it as Jew-Town. The settlement of mostly black residents has by this time largely disappeared, except for the Episcopal Church, which was begun as a mission outpost of Christ Church.

Two other events should be noted as belonging to this Old Mill Days era of history of the island.

The present lighthouse was completed in 1872, so it was there in time to guide the many ships into the harbour and the Frederica river in this important period of time. The first lighthouse had been completed by James Gould in 1811 on a four acre plot donated to the government for the sum of $1.00, by John Couper in 1804. This had served the plantation era of the island. However, when the Confederate troops were forced to evacuate the island in 1862, they destroyed the lighthouse to keep it from being used as a marking point by Federal ships blockading the coast. In the intervening ten years between lighthouses, the four story cotton barn of Retreat Plantation was often used by sailors as a marking point. The new lighthouse of 1872 was built alongside the location of the earlier lighthouse, which foundation ruin may still be seen there.

The other significant event of this era is the rebuilding of the Christ Church building in 1884. The organization of this congregation is old, going back to Charles Wesley and the days of Fort Frederica. The first building of 1820 did not survive its hard use by northern troops during the Civil War, when it was used for many purposes except worship.

St. James Union Church, 1880

Thus after the war it stood derelict and abandoned, while the former members worshipped in homes, as they had no resources for rebuilding their church building. Anson Green Phelps Dodge, Jr. came to visit his father, one of the owners of the mills. Falling in love with the island, and searching in his own life for more meaning than his wealth had already brought him, a dream developed to become the pastor of Christ Church and rebuild its building. When his beautiful wife died in the Orient on their honeymoon, he returned her body to St. Simons Island and built a new Christ Church building in her memory. Here he served as a beloved pastor until his death.

It may be of interest that in this era the Hilton-Dodge Lumber Company of St. Simons Island sawed much of the timber used in the construction of the famous Brooklyn Bridge in New York City in 1878. So this era provided historic timber as did the early plantation days when much of the timber for the ship "Old Ironsides" came from this island and was shipped from this same bluff on the Frederica river.

As the years pass, times and circumstances change, one era turns into another. The best of the timber had been cut, markets changed, companies developed other interests. Gradually the mills slowed in activity and then were abandoned. It had been a great period from about 1874 to 1908, and it must have been with great sadness that people saw its passing. But a new era was at hand. Just as the Indians of old could not imagine the change in their way of life by the coming of the white man from Europe, so the person working at the old saw mill could little imagine the changes to come by the arrival of the automobile.

Ships at Mill Wharf

VII. EARLY RESORT DAYS

The Civil War had brought a great disruption of family and economic life all across Georgia. These hard times and chaotic conditions continued for several years after the war. However, by the eighteen-seventies conditions were taking on more signs of normalcy. People from the mainland cities were beginning to dream of vacations and the cooling breezes of the ocean, and some of them were becoming sufficiently affluent to come to the coast in summer. On St. Simons Island the lighthouse had been rebuilt. The first one had been destroyed during the war to prevent its being a landmark for Federal ships, but now after ten years a new one again began showing its light in 1872. Also here in the south end of the island a pier had been constructed and a village area was developing.

Of course, people coming to the coast of Georgia for its beauty and fair weather was nothing new. The very rich had been doing this for many years. Often a wealthy person would purchase an entire island, or a large portion of one. Here he would build a mansion as a place of retreat from worldly cares. During mild winter and early spring, it was pleasant to entertain friends for hunting, fishing, and lavish dining. In 1886 a group of the nation's most wealthy men purchased Jekyll Island and ran it as a grand private club.

St. Simons Island was one of the few islands where land was not exclusively in the hands of a few people, so was ripe for resort development. On the south end of the island near the pier, summer cottages were built in great numbers. These were largely unsealed, unheated, summer houses built for three months occupancy. People came to Brunswick by train, by carriage, in early autos, and took boats, such as the Emmeline and the Hessie, across to the pier at St. Simons.

It was in this period that the area received widespread publicity of its wonder and beauty with the publication of the poem in 1878 "The Marshes of Glynn" by Sidney Lanier. Mr. Lanier had come to Brunswick in late 1874 to visit in the home of his wife's brother, Mr. Henry Day. Already, Mr. Lanier suffered the beginning of a dread disease (from which he would die in 1881) and arrived in a weakened condition. With the mild winter and early spring, he was soon able to take daily rides, and was greatly thrilled and moved by the beauty and wonder of the marshes. In the spring of 1875 he wrote a poem "The Marshes of Glynn", and a few days later at a meeting of the literary club at the home of Mrs. James M. Couper this poem was read aloud for the first time and from the original manuscript.

Near the St. Simons Island pier a great number of summer houses had been constructed. So many of the

Trolley

summer residents came from Waycross that a section of them became referred to as the "Waycross Colony". With stores and a hotel, this area had become a bustling summer village.

A resort hotel was built on the ocean at the present site of Massengale Park. To transport the guests from the pier, a railway track was laid from the boat dock to the hotel. Open air cars were pulled by a mule; then later by a motorized unit; then still later, this was replaced by an enclosed trolley car. The beach front hotel was owned by the same people as the Oglethorpe Hotel in Brunswick. For summer when hotel occupancy was low in Brunswick, they would move much of the Oglethorpe Hotel furniture to their hotel on St. Simons for the summer, and then move it back to Brunswick for the winter.

bathing 1890's

In 1898 a camp was established near the pier for soldiers fighting in the Spanish-American War. Then for many years after the war, soldiers were sent here for summer camp exercises.

Of course this period of time was largely concurrent with the Old Mill Days at Gascoigne Bluff. Yet on this still largely wilderness island with few improved roads, the business activity of the mills and the resort activity of the beach were largely separate. This is the reason for their being presented as separate eras. They both began in the 1870's. The lumber mills went out of existence about 1908, while the early resort period lasted up through most of the 1920's.

It was with the coming of the coastal highway, the improvement of the automobile roads, the mass production of cars, and finally the building of the causeway making the island accessible to people in automobiles, which brought great changes in the nature of the resort community.

"Double Pen" Cottage
Waycross Colony

VIII. LATER RESORT DAYS

Automobiles, the Causeway, and Sea Island

The early resort period had been largely limited to the people who could come by train and ferry. The resort consisted of wooden buildings clustered near the pier, most of which were boarded up for nine months of the year. The island was still largely wilderness, with few roads.

This picture changes rapidly with the coming of the mass produced automobile and the improvement of roads for these cars. St. Simons Island was about the only one of the Georgia coastal islands still available for development. Most of the islands were the private property of rich people holding them as a private retreat and hunting grounds.

Many persons saw the possibility of development, but the story can best be told in relationship to the vision, imagination, and wise judgement of Howard Coffin.

Mr. Coffin was an automobile engineer in the very early days of the new industry. He was born of Quaker parents on a farm near West Milton, Ohio; attended high school in Ann Arbor, Michigan; then studied engineering at the University of Michigan. He had the vision of producing a low cost car which would sell for less than a thousand dollars and would therefore be available to a mass market.

In 1902 he went to work for the Olds Motor Works of Detroit, thus beginning a career which would soon make him one of the most famous of the automobile builders and very wealthy as well. After Olds decided to stay with the expensive car, he served other companies until he was able to achieve his dream of an inexpensive car to sell to the average man on the street. With the financial backing of the Hudson department stores of Detroit and with their customers in mind for the cars, he brought into being the Hudson car, the first model a four-cylinder roadster selling for $900. This company boomed, and so did his fortunes.

The first visit of Mr. Coffin to the coast of Georgia was in 1910 to attend the Savannah Road Race. Early automobile manufacturers liked to test their latest models in races over winding dirt roads, and the race held at Savannah had attracted wide attention. Mr. and Mrs. Coffin made this trip to watch their cars perform, but making it a vacation trip in a way, coming in a leisurely journey by train. They immediately fell in love with the beauty and history of the Golden Isles of the Georgia coast. Being well able to afford a private island, like many of his rich friends already had, he purchased the 20,000 acres of marsh and highland that made up Sapelo Island from the five families who owned it. Thus, he had a vacation retreat, a showplace to entertain, and a reason to return often to the Georgia coast.

His real importance to St. Simons Island history, however, is the vision he had for development with the coming of the automobile roads. Soon after the end of World War I the mass sales of autos far surpassed the improvement of roads for their travel. Gradually a coastal highway began to inch down from the north, and it was only time until the now U.S. 17 would bring the tourists. He knew that there was money to be made in owning land in strategic places along such a highway, particularly in areas where there could be resort activity. So he purchased many tracts of land.

The other factor in development of St. Simons Island, besides the coastal highway, was the building of a causeway. Imagine autos carrying carloads of people to the island in fifteen minutes, instead of the slow trip by ferry and then the lack of transportation after arriving at the pier!

No one knows who first thought of building a causeway to St. Simons Island. Probably across the years many people thought of this possibility. It has even been suggested that General Oglethorpe may have considered it as an escape avenue for his soldiers and colonists. Yet, the first person to talk about it long and loud enough to get movement in that direction was William T. McCormick in about the year 1920. No one would listen to him at first, but he continued to talk about it so much anyway that many people began to consider him slightly balmy. Finally, he did interest some investors in island property and access by a causeway. Money being so tight they planned for what seemed the shortest, less expensive route, which was from the coastal highway about ten miles north of Brunswick. They actually did begin construction by clearing a road from the highway to the marsh, but then running into difficulty and financial uncertainty, abandoned the project without ever getting out into the marsh.

This beginning, however, had sparked considerable interest in the project and soon popular opinion supported a joint bond issue by the City of Brunswick and Glynn County to provide the funds. With money available it was felt wise to construct it closer to Brunswick, and after consulting with state highway engineers a route was projected. Fortunately, they were wise enough to consult a native son and competent engineer, Mr. F.J. Torras, to check the route and make a survey of the marsh. His recommendation, which was adopted, brought it still another mile closer to the city and several miles closer to the south end of St. Simons. Construction proceeded smoothly, and the causeway was opened on July 11, 1924, with the greatest celebration in Brunswick history. Guests came by train, by boat, by automobile, by horse and buggy. Special trains brought guests from afar. More than 5,000 automobiles crossed the causeway that day; the first of the great parade had reached the island before the last of it had entered the new road. Officials in both high and low positions made long speeches. A great pageant was performed. A huge dinner was served; under old, moss draped live oak trees hundreds of tables were erected and a shore dinner was served to 7,500 visitors.

This easy access to the island was not lost on developer Howard Coffin. He soon purchased the land of former Retreat Plantation on the south end of the island and other tracts. The roads on this still almost wilderness island needed to be improved and new ones were needed. To go to the village and pier it was then necessary to cross to the east side of the island on Demeree road, passing Bloody Marsh, and following the old military road to the south end of the village. So he had a new road cut directly from the causeway to the south end of the island, which he named "Kings Way." He also built Retreat Avenue, a continuation of Frederica road on southward beyond Demeree to the entrance of Retreat Plantation. Here at Retreat he began laying out a golf course. Even though he did not play golf himself, he saw the "potential" in golf course development. He constructed a yacht club here and was in his mind projecting a hotel on the Frederica river.

Mr. Coffin had also purchased an island to the east which had a very fine beach and a short, mud-road causeway which had been dredged up by earlier developers to connect the island to St. Simons. For years this rather barren island had been used for no more than pasture for hogs and goats and other animals. In early days it had been known as Fifth Creek Island. We do not know whether this is from the Creek Indians or had to do with the counting of the numerous creeks. Some navigational maps refer to it as the Isle of Palms. By this time most people called it Long Island. Mr. Coffin at first named it Glynn Isle and later changed it to Sea Island.

A friend who had much experience with real estate development in Florida advised him to abandon his idea of building a big hotel on St. Simons overlooking the inter-coastal waterway. Modern resort hotels were moving to the beaches, their windows overlooking the sea. He agreed that this little island across the marshes would be an ideal place for his development. Envisioned was an eight story, high rise hotel on the beach, with a community of "cottages" surrounding it. This was projected for the middle of the island between 29th and 32nd streets. Grading had already begun when Mr. Coffin started to have second thoughts. What kind of people would come to this resort? What would they want for entertainment? Who would be attracted to purchase the cottages? Would it attract some of the undesirable features already evident at some of the resorts in Florida?

Those who investigated for him in Florida, recommended that they "take it easy". So it was decided to settle for a small, comfortable inn, where people could stay and decide whether they liked the place enough to build a "cottage". The location for the hotel was moved to the south end of the island and was named the "Cloister." Opening celebrations were in October, 1928.

A tremendous publicity department was created, and over the next months were welcomed a continuing parade of tycoons, sportsmen, artists, writers, statesmen, and editors from all over the country. The new, little resort was quickly becoming known. An early achievement came in 1928 when President Calvin Coolidge was persuaded to spend his Christmas holiday with Howard Coffin and to pose for his picture planting an oak tree on the south lawn of the Cloister. This photograph was printed in all the newspapers of the country. Guests today may now see this tree with 53 years of growth. Such publicity allowed the Cloister to have in its first year of operation more bookings than it could handle.

So, with its reputation established, its type of clientele, and the wisdom of staying with a modest resort, the business was able to weather the soon-to-come depression better than most resorts and later, during World War II, was able to continue operation when most hotels had been taken over by the armed services. This small inn, across two rather rickety causeways, was not well suited for government use.

From the beginning, the company sought to attract a special clientele. It did not encourage the guests who wanted gambling, race tracks, and exotic night clubs. Neither did it encourage the social set who once thronged to resorts to show off their jewels and furs. Rather, the publicity department sent letters such as the one to the two thousand members of the Detroit Athletic Club in 1931. It made an appeal to the business man carrying heavy responsibilities to come for old-fashioned simple rest; a place where nerves, minds, and bodies could have complete relaxation that rebuilds: exercise, good food, restful sleep; the sound of waves on the beach and the smell of pine forests in the air. Come here to "find a wealth of romance and history to charm your mind while nature mends jaded nerves."

With that type of appeal, they did come! William Gibbs McAdoo, Mayor Jimmy Walker, Eddie Rickenbacker, Dean Acheson, Arthur Brisbane, Gladys Swarthout, Thomas W. Dewey, Edsel Ford, John D. Rockefeller, Jr., just to name a few.

A young racing pilot, Jimmy Doolittle, came — still years away from his famous bombing run over Tokyo,

Vice-President Alben Barkley spent his honeymoon here. In fact honeymoons became a tradition. In 1981 the count of honeymoon couples, since June 1940, when the count began, passed 27,000. Children and grandchildren of former honeymoon couples are now coming.

President Dwight D. Eisenhower and President Gerald Ford when guests both had live oak trees planted in their honor, as did her majesty Queen Juliana of the Netherlands, when she and her consort Prince Bernhard spent the Easter weekend here in 1952.

In 1931 the nation's most famous playwright, Eugene O'Neill, came seeking a peaceful place to live and work. He built a home on a six lot spread on the ocean at 19th Street. While here he wrote his only comedy, "Ah Wilderness." Although he avoided social life, his presence did attract visitors of similar talents — Somerset Maugham, Sherwood Anderson, Lillian Gish, Bennet Cerf, among others. He kept this home until 1936, the year he was awarded the Nobel prize, when he moved to California, still trying to find the peace of mind he was forever seeking.

Sarah Churchill, daughter of Sir Winston Churchill and an actress of some renown, had been on an American tour in a stock company playing "The Philadelphia Story". After the sixteen week tour closed in Atlanta, she came to the Cloister for some rest, relaxation, and sunshine. With her was a young Englishman, Anthony Beauchamp, a British society photographer specializing in portraits. While here they decided to get married, and on October 17, 1949, they went to Fort Frederica to announce to the press and to the world that they would be married the next day.

In 1927 while the resort was still under construction, a young pilot, Paul Redfern, who was skilled in flying over the north Georgia swamps looking for moonshiners, took off from Sea Island beach in an attempt to solo flight to Brazil. The plane was last seen two hundred miles off the South American coast, but never heard from again.

A young aviation hero, Charles Lindbergh, enroute to Mexico after his famed flight to Paris, had been guests of Mr. Coffin and Mr. Jones, landing in a pasture on nearby Sapelo Island. The trip was memorable for Lindbergh; while in Mexico City he met the ambassador's daughter, Anne Morrow, whom he later was to marry.

In more recent times, newly elected President Jimmy Carter brought together his new Cabinet at the Cloister. Later, when President Carter used Musgrove Plantation, a present day plantation on St. Simons, as a vacation retreat, the Cloister staff provided the household services and food which were needed.

About this same time on the north end of Sea Island near the Hampton river, black men and women had been crowded into cages and loaded aboard ships, where ABC television photographers had found the foliage and the beaches they needed to film Alex Haley's "Roots".

Howard Coffin, who had the vision of this resort development, died in 1937, and the enterprize was carried on by his cousin, Alfred W. Jones, who had long worked with him. The visitor to Christ Church cemetery, after seeing the tombs of the island people featured in the historical novels of Eugenia Price, would do well to also visit the graves of Mr. and Mrs. Coffin. They will see there a somewhat unusual placing of the graves. The plot is a square enclosed by a two foot high tabby wall. The simple gravestones lie flat and are not parallel with the walls but are on a diagonal. This reflects a curious idea of Mr. Coffin. When alive, whenever possible, he slept with his head to the north, for he believed that if he did not, the rotation of the earth had a deleterious effect on the circulation of the blood.

Of course, the Cloister was not the only development in this later resort era. The King and Prince Hotel was built on the beach at St. Simons. There is the more recent Sea Palms resort. Then, there is Epworth-by-the Sea, the conference and program grounds of the South Georgia Conference of the United Methodist Church. Bishop Arthur J. Moore was the moving spirit behind this development. Built on the very historic ground at Gascoigne Bluff — once Hamilton Plantation, then the site of the great sawmills, then a vegetable farm — Methodists and members of many other denominations come together, not only from Georgia, but from all parts of the world. The museum located there is filled with treasures of Methodist history, including two original, handwritten letters of John Wesley. A life-size statue of Bishop Arthur J. Moore, made of wax in London, England, welcomes the visitor to see the vast collection of his momentos and treasures from around the world.

This late resort era continues today, as it blends into the most recent historic era, the Residential Period of the island.

King and Prince — lobby entrance until 1986

IX. THE RESIDENTIAL ERA

In 1961 two authors from Chicago, Eugenia Price and Joyce Blackburn, were on an autographing tour of the south when enroute they visited St. Simons Island. Charmed by its beauty and rich history, they immediately fell in love with it. Later, they were to move here, Eugenia Price writing a trilogy of novels spanning the history of the island. Most of her characters in the Novels — **Lighthouse, New Moon Rising,** and **The Beloved Invader** — were real people, whose graves may be visited in Christ Church cemetery. Those lovely stories brought widespread attention to the history and the beauty of St. Simons Island. Visitors flocked here to see the sights and to visit the graves. Many fell in love with the island and its gentle climate, and they too decided to stay.

The author of this little book first visited St. Simons Island in the spring of 1953. It was a chance visit for sightseeing, but discovering camping permitted in the park just north of the village, we put our belongings in a pup-tent, allowing Mrs. Green and me and our three month old baby, Tom, to sleep in the bed prepared in our car. Fond memories of this place included it on our "search list" in 1978 as we sought the best place of all to retire. St. Simons Island won first choice, and we moved into our new home in the summer of 1980. Within a few weeks the three month old baby of 1953, now an adult, returned for a visit bringing his own 3½ week old baby, Daniel, with him. On October 9, 1980, we all gathered in the front lawn of our home for a ceremony, planting a live oak tree in honor of the visit of the baby in his first weeks of life. The baby will be instructed to return in 80 years as an old man to see how the "Daniel Ross Green Live Oak Tree" is doing as it reaches toward maturity.

This enchantment with the beauty, the history, the

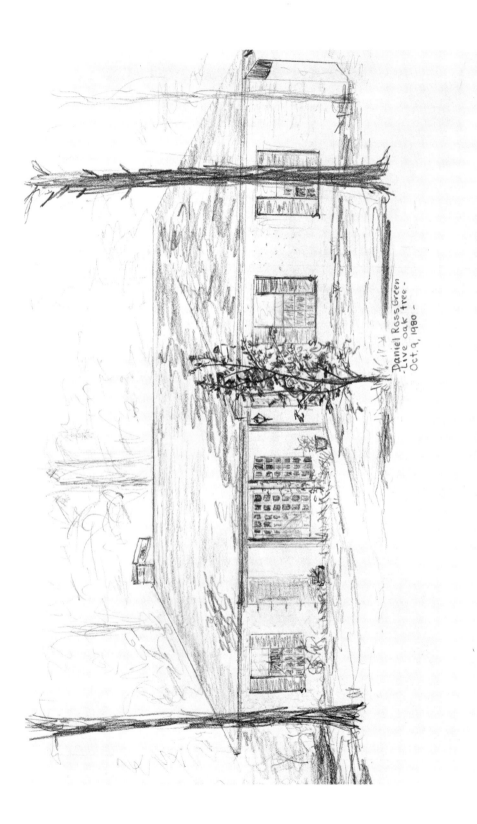

Daniel Ross Green
- Live oak tree -
Oct. 9, 1980 -

loveliness of it as a place to live has attracted hundreds of families. With people living to a more advanced age, and with social security and pensions providing a means of livelihood, it was now possible for the retired to move to a more gentle climate, escaping the bitter cold and the snows of the northlands.

Who can say exactly when this Residential Era began, but it reached something of a floodtide in the seventies. The island population grew from 5,346 in 1960; to 6,818 in 1970; to 9,328 in 1980. Some of these new residents are people with a great deal of talent, adding to the educational and cultural life of the island. Many retirees have spent years in business, medicine, law, the military, and other professions which makes them valuable resource persons for the community.

A symbol of the "new south" and the "Residential Era" of the island was very visible on Saturday, December 13, 1980 when all of Glynn County, Brunswick, St. Simons, Jekyll, gathered for "Mack Mattingly Day". Mr. Mattingly, a resident of St. Simons Island, had just been elected United States Senator from Georgia. He is the first Republican to be elected to the Senate from Georgia since Reconstruction days. He had defeated the incumbent, Herman Talmadge, a family long entrenched in Georgia political life. Coming from Indiana twenty years before, a business man in Brunswick, active in Republican politics, he was now becoming the first U.S. Senator from this area. Of course his election was in the wake of the Ronald Reagan presidential landslide and partly as a result of ethics questions about his opponent who seemed to have an overcoat with a magic pocket that "never ran out of money." Fluke or not, St. Simons Island and the entire area felt honored to have a resident in the U.S. Senate. So, organized by the Chamber of Commerce, and supported by almost everyone, Republican and Democrat alike, there was a great parade, speech making, and a barbecue on "Mack Mattingly Day". This, I think, is a symbol of the changing south, and new attitudes which come by an influx of population, and therefore of the Residential Era.

The "developers" have taken advantage of this southern migration as addition after addition of real estate has been platted into residential lots, lovely homes constructed, apartments and condominiums planned. The price of land has kept up with inflation, sparked with this kind of demand. In the 1924-26 first development on Sea Island, an undeveloped corner lot on the beach sold for $200, with an interior lot going for $100. In 1980 the summer real estate folder lists a 150 foot ocean frontage lot at $325,000 and interior lots on the Sea Island Drive at $150,000. "Cottages" at Sea Island have a unique numbering system. Numbers are not according to location, but in chronological order of when they were built. Those with low numbers date back into the late twenties. Those under construction in 1980 include #376 by Judge Griffin B. Bell and #381 by James R. Hewell, Jr., who at 25th Street and the Ocean is building the largest "cottage" on Sea Island. Development is continuing northward of 36th Street and also on St. Simons around the Sea Island Golf Club and the St. Simons Island Club. 1980 prices of these lots were generally in the forty-five to fifty-five thousand dollar price range.

Growth is most likely to continue at a rapid rate as the southern migration continues. There are still miles and miles of wilderness areas on the north end of St. Simons Island ready for development. Hampton Point at the extreme north end on the Hampton river has already been platted and is for sale. A large condominium unit is also projected in this area. With this the residents of the island express concern for the orderly growth, proper zoning, and the preservation of the history and beauty of St. Simons. There are projections for improvement of the causeway. There are those who express the need for a second causeway to the north end of the island. There are those who debate the features of a Master Plan for Development.

Yet, who can really fortell the future? When will this present Residential Era be replaced with another? What will it be? Only those of you who are reading this sometime in the 21st century may know.

As to the far future, we even more "look through a glass darkly". If some scientists are correct that a warming trend of the earth began about 1920, a gradual melting of the glaciers may cause the island to disappear in a thousand years or so. If the cycles within cycles of weather make the trend the other way to be colder, we may then be part of the mainland with other emerging islands to the east.

None of us can know this, for a thousand years or so is a long time in our span of life; yet we know that:

"A thousand years in Thy sight,
are but as yesterday when it is past."

SUGGESTIONS FOR FURTHER READING

(For those who wish to study the various historic eras in more detail, here are a few suggested books. This is not a complete bibliography. These and many other titles may be found on the shelves of the local bookstores and libraries.)

I.   The Island and the Indians

    1. Count D. Gibson, *Sea Island of Georgia*, University of Georgia Press, 1948.

    2. National Geographic Magazine, "Sea Island", March, 1971 pp. 366-393.

    3. Mildred & John Teal, *Portrait of an Island,* Antheneum, N.Y. 1964, (the land and wildlife of a Sea Island — specifically about Sapelo Island.)

II. The Spanish Missions

    1. John Tate Lanning, *The Spanish Missions of Georgia*, University of N.C. Press 1935.

    2. Margaret Davis Cate, *Our Todays and Yesterdays*, Reprint Company, Spartensburg, S.C. 1979, from 1930 edition.

III. The English Period

    1. Trevor R. Reese, *Frederica Colonial Fort and Town*, Ft. Frederica Assn., 1969.

    2. Frances L. Mitchell, *Georgia Land and People*, University of Georgia, 1900, Reprint Company, Spartensburg, S.C. 1974.

IV. Early Plantation Era

    1. Caroline Couper Lovell, *The Golden Isles of Georgia*, 1932.

    2. Eugenia Price, *Lighthouse*, (an historical novel), Lippincott 1971.

    3. Frances Anne Kemble ("Fanny" Kemble), *Journal of a Residence on a Georgia Plantation 1838-1839*, Reprint Knopf, 1961.

    4. Bessie Lewis, *Patriarchial Plantations of St. Simons Island* 1974.

    5. Burnette Vanstory, *Georgia's Land of the Golden Isles,* University of Georgia Press, 1956.

V. Plantations in Maturity and Decline

1. Margaret Davis Cate, *Early Days of Coastal Georgia*, Fort Frederica Association, Gallery Press, N.Y. 1955.

2. Mrs. Frances B. Leigh (daughter of Fanny Kemble), *Ten Years on a Georgia Plantation Since the War,* London 1883, Reprinted Negro University Press, N.Y. 1969.

3. Eugenia Price, *New Moon Rising* (an historical novel) Lippincott, 1969.

VI. Old Mill Days 1874-1908

1. Abbie Fuller Graham, *Old Mill Days*, by the St. Simons Public Library, 1976.

2. Eugenia Price, *The Beloved Invader,* (an historical novel), Lippincott, 1965.

VII. Early Resort Days

1. Articles and newspaper clippings reprinted in the scrapbook of the St. Simons Library, included in Fuller, *Old Mill Days* referred to above.

2. Frances Peabody McKay, *More Fun than Heaven* (about the Waycross Colony), Valkyrie Press, St. Petersburg, Florida.

VIII. Later Resort Days

1. Harold H. Martin, *This Happy Isle,* (the story of Sea Island) 1978.

2. Opening Program *Brunswick — St. Simons Highway,* July 11, 1924, Official program by Womens Club of Brunswick.

3. Newspaper articles about the Causeway opening. Reprinted in *Old Mill Days,* the library scrapbook referred to above.

4. Anthony Hearn, *Epworth-by-the-Sea, "The Early Years"* Archives of History, South Georgia Conference, United Methodist Church, 1980.